Literature and Religion

"David Jasper's fascinating dialogue with Ou Guang-an vividly materializes the dialogic space between literature and religion, East and West. It would be difficult to find one who has contributed more to stimulate the interdisciplinary studies of theology and literature."
—Yang Huilin, Distinguished Professor of Comparative Literature and Religious Studies, Renmin University of China

"This remarkably adventurous book has become possible because two longstanding friends learned to trust one another. Its readers will find themselves indebted to both the authors for their courtesy to one another and the expectations of care and insight they generate in those willing to embark on comparable studies!"
—Ann Loades, Professor Emerita of Divinity, University of Durham, and Honorary Professor in the School of Divinity, University of St Andrews

"Spiritual values connect religion and literature as manifestations of what is at the core of our humanity, even though the forms of manifestation and the emphases in different cultures may differ from one to the other. Through a series of dialogues and exchanges, David Jasper and Ou Guang-an explore those spiritual values in this fascinating book, *Literature and Religion*, and offer us much to learn, contemplate, and celebrate."
—Zhang Longxi, author of *Allegoresis: Reading Canonical Literature East and West*

"To read this fascinating book is to overhear a gracious, informed, and honest conversation between friends whose life experiences could scarcely be more different. But in that difference, and in the quality of that friendship and the willingness to find seek out new understandings, there is profound revelation which we are privileged to share. Through the translation of literature in its widest sense, the cultures and religions of China and 'the West' are mutually illuminated."
—Alison Jack, Senior Lecturer in Bible and Literature, Assistant Principal of New College, University of Edinburgh

"The interdisciplinary encounter between literature and religion is given new form and vitality in this lively dialogue between two scholars from very different cultural contexts. Their conversation draws the reader in enabling them to explore unfamiliar territory and also rediscover a compelling

strangeness within familiar literary texts. There are many treasures to be found here."
—Heather Walton, Professor of Theology and Creative Practice, University of Glasgow

"If there is ever a time for a new way of intercultural dialogue, it is now, as the world shrinks and divides in equal measures. Jasper and Ou model for us just such a way. The conversations here, going well beyond comparative studies, are the very 'enactment of reciprocity,' conducted in the spirit of unconditional hospitality, and yielding insights germane to not only China and the West, but all sides questioning our shared religious concerns."
—Andrew Hass, Reader in Religion, University of Stirling

Literature and Religion

A DIALOGUE BETWEEN CHINA AND THE WEST

David Jasper
Ou Guang-an

☙PICKWICK Publications • Eugene, Oregon

LITERATURE AND RELIGION
A Dialogue between China and the West

Copyright © 2020 David Jasper and Ou Guang-an. All rights reserved. Except for brief quotations in critical publications or reviews, no part of this book may be reproduced in any manner without prior written permission from the publisher. Write: Permissions, Wipf and Stock Publishers, 199 W. 8th Ave., Suite 3, Eugene, OR 97401.

Pickwick Publications
An Imprint of Wipf and Stock Publishers
199 W. 8th Ave., Suite 3
Eugene, OR 97401

www.wipfandstock.com

PAPERBACK ISBN: 978-1-5326-5218-9
HARDCOVER ISBN: 978-1-5326-5219-6
EBOOK ISBN: 978-1-5326-5220-2

Cataloguing-in-Publication data:

Names: Jasper, David, author. | Ou, Guang'an, author.

Title: Literature and religion : a dialogue between China and the West / David Jasper and Ou Guang-an.

Description: Eugene, OR : Pickwick Publications, 2020 | Includes bibliographical references and index.

Identifiers: ISBN 978-1-5326-5218-9 (paperback) | ISBN 978-1-5326-5219-6 (hardcover) | ISBN 978-1-5326-5220-2 (ebook)

Subjects: LCSH: Religion and literature. | Religion in literature. | East and West.

Classification: PN49 .J38 2020 (print) | PN49 .J38 (ebook)

Manufactured in the U.S.A.   OCTOBER 6, 2020

Table of Contents

Acknowledgments ix

Introduction (David Jasper and Ou Guang-an) 1

From East to West

1. Literary Similarities and Cultural Differences: A Comparative Study of *Zhuangzi* and the Book of Job (Ou Guang-an) 13
2. The Book of Job and *Zhuangzi*: A Response (David Jasper) 29
3. A Textual and Cross-Cultural Investigation of "Fate" in Thomas Hardy's *Tess of the D'Urbervilles* (Ou Guang-an) 34
4. Thomas Hardy and the Conflict of Cultures: A Response (David Jasper) 56
5. Religious Perspectives in Yeats's Poetry (Ou Guang-an) 61
6. Response to Yeats: Sinking in on Truth (David Jasper) 82

From West to East

7. Issues in Sino-Christian Theology (David Jasper) 89
8. Response to Issues in Sino-Christian Theology (Ou Guang-an) 102
9. Towards a Reading of Lu Xun (David Jasper) 108
10. Response to the Reading of Lu Xun (Ou Guang-an) 118
11. Seeking Christian Theology in Modern Chinese Fiction: An Exercise for Sino-Christian Theology (David Jasper) 123

TABLE OF CONTENTS

12. Response to Seeking Christian Theology in Modern Chinese Fiction (Ou Guang-an) 138

Concluding Conversations

13. Concluding Reflections (David Jasper) 145

14. Final Remarks (Ou Guang-an) 153

15. Suggested Further Reading 161

Bibliography 163

Index 171

Acknowledgments

THE AUTHORS WOULD LIKE to thank New College in the University of Edinburgh for granting us the opportunity to work together for a period of six months in 2019 so that these "conversations" might bear fruit in this book. We thank our mutual friend Dr Daniel Yeung of the Institute of Sino-Christian Studies in Tao Fong Shan, Hong Kong, who first introduced us to one another. Words can hardly express our thanks to Dr Heather Barcroft for her highly professional and extraordinarily patient help in bringing our chapters together in a clear and coherent way. Finally, thanks are due to our two families, who bore with our endless discussions and hours hidden away in studies and libraries.

Introduction

David Jasper and Ou Guang-an

In 1901 the English sinologist Herbert Giles published his *History of Chinese Literature* as a volume in Heinemann's popular series of Short Histories of the Literatures of the World. In his first sentence Giles claims that this was the first attempt "in any language, including Chinese, to produce a history of Chinese literature."[1] Although some English literature, not least the works of William Shakespeare, and the Bible were known in Chinese in the nineteenth century, there was relatively little literary exchange between Chinese and Western[2] culture until the twentieth century, during which the political and cultural changes in China impeded much exchange until the very end of the century.

From the beginning of the present century things began to change rapidly. Kam Louie of the University of Hong Kong and editor of the *Cambridge Companion to Modern Chinese Culture* (2008) writes:

> Interest in Chinese literature, philosophy, cinema, *qigong*, and other cultural artefacts around the world is stronger now than ever before. There has been a plethora of books about Chinese culture published in anglophone countries and a steady increase in students enrolling in courses on Chinese language and civilization.[3]

Many Chinese students come to study at universities in Europe, North America, Australia, and New Zealand, while academics and students from these countries are now welcomed to teach and study at Chinese

---

1. Giles, *History of Chinese Literature*, v.

2. The term "Western" we acknowledge is problematic, as if the world was divided between China and "the West." Given that this book is a conversation between a Chinese and a British scholar, we use the term advisedly and in full recognition of its limitations.

3. Kam Louie, "Defining Modern Chinese Culture," 1.

universities. But the conversations in this book are not simply literary. Its authors met and became friends while studying in Hong Kong at the Institute of Sino-Christian Studies at Tao Fong Shan, a Christian center founded in 1930 by the Norwegian missionary Karl Ludwig Reichelt to promote dialogue between Buddhism and Christianity. "Religion" is not an easy word to define, but it cannot be easily dismissed in intercultural literary discussions.

Kam Louie acknowledges that the opening up of Chinese culture in Western minds inevitably has a historical dimension "with contemporary culture reproducing and modernizing relics of China's historical past."[4] The rapid development of Confucius Institutes, sponsored by the Chinese government in universities around the world is indicative of a self-conscious connection between contemporary culture and education and two thousand years of the study of the writings of Confucius in China. Whether "Confucianism" is a religion is highly debated, but certainly the missionary and scholar James Legge, the first Professor of Chinese Language and Literature in the University of Oxford clearly regarded it as a religion in his influential work *The Religions of China: Confucianism and Taoism Described and Compared with Christianity* (1880). In the West, on the other hand, it is clear that the Bible has continued to exercise huge influence in literature and culture far beyond the limits of religious belief. Our conversations reflect this broad sense of "religion" in culture and the role of literature in its expression.

The chapters and responses in this book are by way of a self-conscious experiment. They are offered in the form of a dialogue between two scholars within the humanities in China and the United Kingdom. Ou Guang-an is a professor of English at Shihezi University, Xinjiang in the People's Republic of China, at the time of writing also a Visiting Scholar in the University of Edinburgh. David Jasper is Emeritus Professor and formerly Professor of Literature and Theology at the University of Glasgow in Scotland. He has also taught for many years at Renmin University of China in Beijing. They met in Hong Kong some years ago, and this book is the fruit of many discussions and a growing friendship, something that lies at the heart of all good academic discussions

No-one can deny that both China and the West (we will keep to that term as a useful umbrella for the culture of Europe and the broader English speaking world) have ancient cultures that are deeply *literary* in forms of

---

4. Kam Louie, "Defining Modern Chinese Culture," 2.

Introduction

poetry and narrative. While the concept of the Axial Age as proposed by Karl Jaspers in his book *The Origin and Goal of History* (1949)[5] is debated as a "myth" it is still powerful in such influential works as Robert N. Bellah's *Religion in Human Evolution* (2011). Implicitly our conversations still acknowledge the power of Jaspers's vision. In the culture of both China and the West we can discuss the "novel" or different kinds of fiction that are profoundly embedded in our histories and yet have the power to speak beyond that embeddedness. Cultures, like people, can converse with one another through their literatures. The matter of religion or theology, on the other hand, is much more problematic. Our assumptions about religion in this book begin largely (though by no means exclusively) in the "Christian West," though this might better be described as a culture that is immersed on many levels with the thought and literature of the Bible, both in matters of belief and in literary and philosophical discussion. China, in this respect, is more difficult and far more complicated than the term "Confucianism" can often seem. A simple and straightforward way to summarize the major influence on the Chinese people's minds and practice, in tradition and in general terms, is by the so-called "three religions" (Confucianism, Buddhism and Daoism), but none of them has occupied such an essentially religious or theological position as that of Christianity and the religions of the Bible in the West. We will be addressing the issue of "religion" in China, and how that word is to be understood in due course. Herbert Giles was dismissive of religion within ancient Chinese culture, once describing "China's greatest men [as] rationalists at heart."[6] Nothing, of course, is ever that simple.

Our conversations, we readily assert, have taken place largely in the context of the relationship between literature *and* religion. From the outset it should be clear that we have found time and again that there are profound differences between us, often not understood by either of us in their entirety, and that these differences should not be underestimated or ironed out in any superficial way. Rather it is from the very acknowledgment of such deep differences that true and trusting friendships can grow in an atmosphere of respect and tolerance that allow dialogue and conversation without demanding the kind of agreement which usually means the rough appropriation of one side by the other. This we have steadfastly tried to avoid. Let each be true to themselves, and perhaps the best we can hope

---

5. Anticipated by the now-forgotten John Stuart Stuart-Glennie in 1873.
6. Giles, *Travels of Fa-hsien*, ix.

for is a kind of "poetics" that acknowledges diversity without fundamental disagreement.[7]

Of continuing importance for Christian theological reflection is George Lindbeck's now quite old book *The Nature of Doctrine* (1984). From Lindbeck's argument we might propose a "cultural linguistic" model for religious understanding in which "the cognitive aspect, while often important, is not primary."[8] Rather imaginative literature, refusing the notion that all religions are basically similar,[9] and unwilling to tolerate abstractions, draws upon religious symbolisms whereby "the basic patterns of religion are interiorized, exhibited, and transmitted." What then becomes crucial is the telling of a story which "gains power and meaning insofar as it is embodied in the total gestalt of community life and action."[10] We begin to find that we are now talking on common ground, whether Chinese or English, and as we set aside for a moment the theological matter of the "transcendent God," Lindbeck's liberal proposals suggest how such a linguistic-cultural model of religion as found in the literatures of any culture might relate in one way or another to liberationist critiques of all forms rather than simply remain complicit with Western philosophical ontologies and ideologies with their often colonial and imperial structures of power and domination.

This, then, is a helpful time for more liberal forms of Western religious thinking as this is a moment in history when the literature of ancient as well as contemporary China is beginning to become more widely available to Western readers, essentially for the first time. This literary voice of China is in no way to be confused by Western readers with a writer like the Japanese novelist Shūsako Endō (and his best known work *Silence* [English translation, 1969]), not only because they are Chinese (a distinction alarmingly still lacking clarity in some Western readers) but also because none of the Chinese writers we read in this book are Christian, unlike Endō. The shift that is of importance to us has been suggested by the Chinese scholar (now working in Hong Kong and formerly in the USA), Zhang Longxi in his book *From Comparison to World Literature* (2015) where he argues that the assumptions of comparative literature, which have hitherto been largely Western, are now expanding to a more genuinely global model that takes more seriously the place of Chinese literature with its very different history

---

7. See further, Jasper et al., *Poetics of Translation*.
8. Lindbeck, *Nature of Doctrine*, 35.
9. Lindbeck, *Nature of Doctrine*, 41.
10. Lindbeck, *Nature of Doctrine*, 36.

and cultural context. In literary terms, and despite all other differences, we are all members of one global family.

To adapt an image of Maurice Blanchot, religion may then be discussed within the "space of literature" with a passion that is without religious or theological pretensions, but still demands a response from religion.[11] It is not, of course, the task of literature to articulate or construct any theology, Christian or otherwise. The novelist, poet or creative writer is not in any sense a theologian or even a religious thinker by another name. But, the creative writer may begin to explore anew the suffering, joyful narratives and moments in human experience that may prompt afresh the task of theology with its different creativities and purposes, Christian or otherwise.

It is in this light that we approach the texts, Western and Chinese, which are discussed in this book. We began with the agreement that each would read and comment on texts and ideas drawn from deep within the other's culture, prompting a response from within the parent culture in each case. (One major limitation is that all our reading is in English and not in Chinese.) We recognize that whether we are reading W. B. Yeats, Thomas Hardy, or Lu Xun, we are confronted by the question as to what is meant by the "spirit" or "soul" of a people, and we are also confronted by the fundamental matter of truth, a term that is universally hard pressed in our modern political and global culture of "post-truth." What will become clear from our discussions is that it is, of course, perfectly possible for a Chinese scholar to read Thomas Hardy's *Tess of the D'Urbervilles* (1891) or for a British scholar to read Lu Xun's novella "The Real Story of Ah-Q" (1923), but each does so with a perhaps inevitable sense of alienation and even disorientation. It is precisely this that prompts and demands serious dialogue and discussion. We have found that we need each other in our meticulous task of mutual and cross-cultural understanding. This is not a task that can be done alone. Of course it would be true to say that the contemporary Chinese novelists read here (by David Jasper)—Yu Hua, Yan Lianke, Sheng Keyi and others—all elicit echoes from other literatures, not least the literature of the West. For example, Yan Lianke's *Serve the People!* (2007) certainly begs comparison with Jaroslav Hasek's comic satire *The Good Soldier Švejk*. This is an instance of intertextual literary resonance that cuts across all cultural and historical barriers in literature.

But, of course, to say that something reminds you of something else is not to admit that they are the same. Nevertheless, it is still a starting point

---

11. Blanchot, *Space of Literature*.

for understanding and conversation. An intrinsic part of the writing of this book has been the questions we have been prompted to ask each other. Often they have arisen out of an admission of ignorance, for what is obvious in one culture may be utterly remote from another. These are questions that must be posed in a genuine spirit of enquiry, and very often we have had to be content with the response, "Yes, I *think* I see what you mean." That is as good, sometimes, as it can get, but that is at least something—a start. And so all conclusions must be reached with an awareness of the matter of *tolerance*—something which every culture has sometimes found difficult, however liberal or open it thinks itself to be. And more often than not it is in matters relating to sex or religion (two large preoccupations of all literature in the end) that cultures are most hesitant, private and nervous.

One of the most widely read cultural critics in both the West and China today is Terry Eagleton, whose relationship with religion has always been edgy and complicated. In one of his recent books, *Culture and the Death of God* (2015), Eagleton addresses the *superfluous* nature of religious belief, either because it is regarded as increasingly irrelevant (in the West), or as presenting a difficulty to a ruling ideology (as in contemporary China). Eagleton writes:

> If religious faith were to be released from the burden of furnishing social orders with a set of rationales for their existence, it might be free to rediscover its true purpose as a critique of all such politics. In this sense, its superfluity might prove its salvation.[12]

In one sense, as religion becomes less important it begins to rediscover its true critical voice. And that critical voice can be heard in many of the texts from literature that we will be reading in this book—texts that sometimes seemingly ignore religion or are at odds with it as it is established in society. Or is it that we are finding this a way, by literature, more simply (and mysteriously) to recover our true humanity across every potential boundary of division—cultural, racial, religious and so on. Literature can help us to loosen the ties of religion from its particular philosophical and theological roots, noting, with Eagleton, that, for example, Christian theologies are often "too indebted to neoplatonic and ahistorical understandings of transcendence to be of use for . . . Christian praxis."[13] The literary freedoms of every culture, being more inclined to recognize a universal

---

12. Eagleton, *Culture and the Death of God*, 207.
13. Eagleton, *Culture and the Death of God*, 206.

INTRODUCTION

rather than a culturally specific community of texts, help us move towards such freedoms.

We realize, of course, that such reflections pose many difficult and complex questions for philosophy, theology, cultural studies and literature itself. A dialogue or conversation such as is found in this book will often pose more, and more interdisciplinary questions than it can possibly answer. But such a conversation is itself a kind of *praxis*—a practical discussion between friends who are willing to try and learn and discover their fundamental commonality in a world which is all too often deeply divided in so many ways. Here there has been no motive of coercion or desire for conversion. We have tried to respect the other's views while not denying our own. The truth perhaps is that such dialogical conversations are finally more important and more humane than all dogma, doctrine or assertion.

"Dialogue" indeed is the very word to properly describe the whole process of writing this book. It begins in actual enthusiastic dialogues and discussions held in a café near Waverley Station in Edinburgh or a seminar room in the University of Glasgow. Such dialogues are continued when we are drafting our own chapters and responses to each other. Behind all these dialogues, there is possibly a further intended dialogue that is meant to take place between we two authors and our readers. All these dialogues, in one way or another, fall into the paradigm of conversation between oneself and the other, and finally between oneself as another.[14]

With this appears the urgent and intriguing question: why do we have to converse or make dialogue? Why does David Jasper have to read the stories of Lu Xun and Ou Guang-an read the poems of Yeats? The answer is, finally, to know more and to communicate better. In the story of Babel (Gen 11:1–9), the paradox, it seems, is that it is only by not knowing (God "confused" language so that the Babel tower could not be built) that people began to know themselves. In the book of Job, by questioning the way of God to "good people," Job finally came to understand his own limitations and foolishness in trying to know the one who cannot be known. In the *Odyssey*, when Hermes is plucking the moly and pointing out the nature of the plant to Odysseus, it is seen that the god thus helps Odysseus to save his companions who had been changed by Circe into pigs. Instead of showing his magic power as one of the Olympian gods, Hermes is actually showing Odysseus the way of knowing himself.[15] In an ancient Chinese fable (with

---

14. Ricoeur, *Oneself as Another*.
15. Homer, *Odyssey*, 163.

universal resonances), five blind men, when they are touching each part of an elephant, tell each other that what each one sees is the whole picture of an elephant. Paradoxically, Laozi argues that the Way in Daoism can be known, but the known Way is not the normal Way. While Confucius taught his disciples that if you know something you do indeed know something, but if you do not know something definitely you cannot claim that you know something. Thus it can easily be seen that knowing is not an easy thing. If to know oneself is indeed difficult, then what is the need to know "the other"? The answer can also be easy: to know "the other" means to achieve a better understanding of oneself, and, indeed no-one is an island. As literature is universal and yet is so profoundly embedded in a certain culture, so it may be that what is glaringly obvious to one person simply passes another by without notice. It is only when one points out what is "obvious" to himself but not the other that one begins to achieve a better understanding or a fuller picture of the whole "elephant." Meanwhile, in the conversation, when one tells a story, the other may immediately echo a similar story in another culture. For example, the "prodigal son" image in George Eliot's *Adam Bede* prompts a similar image in *The Story of the Stone* (*The Dream of Red Mansions*), a classical Chinese novel, though with radical difference in religious and culturally specific connotations. The culturally specific difference and the possible similarity in narration archetypes are the very fabric that adds sparkle to our conversations. In the process of exchange there is an inevitable act of one trying to enter into another culture by familiar references and echoes. This process of cultural exchange immediately evokes in both of us George Steiner's proposal of four phases in translation. The process of translation lies at the heart of all conversations, together with the question, what is, after all translation, after Babel?

In today's "postmodern" world it is easy to become "lost in translation" and to lose the power to communicate with others in a quite different cultural environment. In all our conversations and discussions we have found that the culturally specific phenomenon can be so profoundly embedded that the transition from one cultural context to another can be finally impossible. There are times when the cultural specific phenomenon in literature, for example the iambic pentameter in a Shakespearean sonnet or a fixed rhyming tune in a poem of the Tang Dynasty, is ultimately utterly untranslatable, reflecting Robert Frost's words that "poetry is something lost in translation."[16] However, despite all our cultural differences, we did

16. See also Merrill, "Lost in Translation."

INTRODUCTION

not finally lose ourselves in "translation," because we continued to recognize the differences in translating from culture to culture without demanding an absolute agreement. The dialogical principle held in all our conversations. That lies at the very heart of the book that is to follow.

From East to West

1

Literary Similarities and Cultural Differences

A Comparative Study of *Zhuangzi* and the Book of Job

OU GUANG-AN

Introduction

THIS CHAPTER WILL COMPARE two ancient texts from different cultures, examining both their literary similarities and their cultural differences. These texts are *Zhuangzi*, a foundational work for Taoism in ancient China, and the biblical Book of Job.

Zhuangzi (or *Chuang Tzu*) is a collection of essays and stories in thirty-three chapters and is thought to have been written by the ancient Chinese philosopher Zhuangzi and his disciples in the middle of the Warring States Period (ca. 300 BCE). The received text is the version of Guo Xiang (d. 312 CE), who further contributes a dense and philosophical treatise by way of commentary.[1] It is considered with the *Daodejing* (or *Tao Te Ching*) by Laozi to be one of the two classics that establish the fundamental conceptions of Taoism in China. Together with Confucianism, Taoism (道家) was originally a Chinese school of philosophy with an initial emphasis on naturally following the Tao ("道," literally "the Way") that is the ultimate source and aim. Furthermore one is passively to accept what happens, that

---

1. Kern, "Early Chinese Literature," 73–75.

is, literally, "doing nothing" (*wu wei*).[2] Compared with other ancient classics such as the *Analects* and *Mencius*, *Zhuangzi* changes the literary form by frequently employing fictional narratives as illustrations of philosophical reflections. In order to explain the concept of accepting what heaven gives you or what happens to you and then doing nothing, there are several stories about characters who suffer deprivation or physical deformities. Such characters do not question the way of heaven and simply receive what has happened to them with acceptance and fortitude. In these stories, there are also dramatic dialogues between the suffering character and his friends. Reflected in these dialogues are different attitudes towards life understood as indicating the distinctions between Taoism and different voices such as are to be found in Confucian or other schools. But a great deal can be learnt about the origins of Taoism from these dialogues in *Zhuangzi*.

Similarly, in the biblical book of Job there is the story of a character, Job, who is deprived of his family and wealth and suffers terrible physical hardships. There are several dialogues between Job and his "comforters" representative of different voices or values and it is only after these dialogues that the voice of God reveals itself at the end of the book. Therefore it is valuable to compare *Zhuangzi* with the book of Job both for their thematic similarities and for their differences.

However, cross-cultural studies remind us that comparisons of texts from different cultural and religious backgrounds should be made with exceptional care. In such studies an openness to others and dialogue are most important for proper understanding before conclusions are too hastily reached. As a background to this chapter, therefore, I will draw upon the dialogical principles in the critical writings of the Russian philosopher and literary critic Mikhail Bakhtin.[3] Important also will be the principles of the phenomenon that in recent years has emerged and become known as Scriptural Reasoning. This began in the early 1990s in the comparative reading of sacred texts by Christian, Jewish and Islamic scholars as "a kind of depth-historiography" intended to "transform polar opposites into dialogical pairs."[4] That is to say, the understanding and interpretation of one classical text could be open to the other in order to enrich understanding

---

2. Unlike Confucianism, which has a similarly huge influence on Chinese culture and thought but remains essentially a cultural or philosophical ideology, Taoism was developed into two orientations: a philosophical one (道家思想) and a religious one (道教).

3. See, Bakhtin, *Dialogic Imagination*; Todorov, *Mikhail Bakhtin*.

4. Peter Ochs, quoted in Yang, "Possibilities and Values," 163.

through a dialogue between differences and similarities. At the same time, such dialogical re-readings of classical texts suggest reflections upon contemporary issues. By analyzing stories in *Zhuangzi* and the book of Job, it is my hope to shed some light on our understanding of some of today's urgent issues in an age of multiculturalism and cultural exchange.

The Stories

Zhuangzi is not only a philosophical or a religious text. It also contains profoundly beautiful poetic narratives that are reflective of Taoist wisdom and teaching. Sometimes stories are employed to reflect a particular aspect of Zhuangzi's ideas and of particular interest is that known as the "deprivation story."

Here is one example. In Book VI of *Zhuangzi* (entitled "The Way of the Great Teacher"), there is a story about Ziyu, who is deformed and deprived by heaven. The four wise men Zisi, Ziyu, Zili and Zilai become good friends because they share the same idea of "how death and birth, living on and disappearing, compose the one body." Sometime later Ziyu becomes grotesquely deformed and Zisi goes to ask about his friend. Here is the translation by the nineteenth-century missionary and sinologist James Legge (1815–1897) in his late contribution in 1891 to Max Müller's great work *Sacred Books of the East*:

> He was a crooked hunchback; his five viscera were squeezed into the upper part of his body; his chin bent over his navel; his shoulder was higher than his crown; on his crown was an ulcer pointing to the sky; his breath came and went in gasps.[5]

Before we begin a detailed discussion of this passage, we should first explain the reasons for choosing Legge's old translation. Firstly, although there are a number of more recent translations of *Zhuangzi* (e.g., Burton Watson, Wang Rongpei), Legge's translation remains the first important scholarly translation which maintains its authoritative position. Secondly, as a Christian missionary, Legge's translation of *Zhuangzi* reflected his cultural and religious difficulties when facing Chinese Taoist philosophy and Christianity and the Bible.

Although afflicted with this terrible deformity, Ziyu does not question the ways of heaven. Instead he praises the Creator who had made him the

---

5. Zhuangzi, *Writings of Kwang-sze*, in Müller, *Sacred Books of the East*, 247.

deformed object that he is, easy in his mind and making no complaint at all. He even limps to a well and looks at himself, praising the Creator again. When his friend asks him whether he hates his condition or not, Ziyu replies that he does not even though his body would soon begin to decay and die. After all, he might then be reborn in wonderful ways. Thus following the flow of nature he can transcend both joy and sorrow:

> If He were to transform my left arm into a cock, I should be watching with it the time of the night; if He were to transform my right arm into a cross-bow, I should then be looking for a Hsiao to (bring down and) roast; if He were to transform my rump-bone into a wheel, and my spirit into a horse, I should then be mounting it, and would not change it for another steed.[6]

Ziyu, then, never challenges the ways of the Creator and never complains about his condition. Zhuangzi thus reflects a perfect Taoist attitude toward life and death: when one has received what one has to do, there is the time to do it; submission to what happens to you is the highest priority; when we do what the time requires us to do and when we show submission, there is felt neither joy nor sorrow. This kind of state, according to Ziyu (that is, according to Zhuangzi), is a perfect state to which the ancients aspired. In the end, Ziyu admits that, since "creatures cannot overcome Heaven (the inevitable) is a long-acknowledged fact, why should I hate my condition?" Obviously the conclusion for Ziyu is that when you are faced with illness or misfortune, heaven or the Creator destines you for that condition; humankind cannot overcome heaven. Submission then is the only response.

Here we may take a moment to discuss the position of James Legge, from whose translation of *Zhuangzi* this paper takes its quotations. After more than thirty years as a missionary in China, in 1876 Legge became the first Professor of Chinese Language and Literature at Oxford University. In the above quotations, I suggest that Legge is engaging in a kind of scriptural

---

6. Zhuangzi, *Writings of Kwang-sze,* in Müller, *Sacred Books of the East,* 247–48. In this quoted passage there is a controversial interpretation: "On the crown of his head was an ulcer pointing to the sky." The original Chinese is 句 赘 指 天. According to various authoritative versions, its basic meaning is "the hair bun in the back of his head is pointing to the sky." Here Legge may have misunderstood the original text. Zhao Jing has recently suggested that Legge's translation of *Zhuangzi* is rather inferior in quality to his translation of *Daodejing* because he lacked a competent native scholar to assist him. This Legge himself admits. See Jing, "A Study, of the 'Preface' and 'Introduction' to James Legge's *Texts of Taoism*," in Jasper, *Poetics,* 98. However, the sense is certainly unclear. A more recent translation suggests, "his neck-bone pointed up to the sky" (Chuang Tzu, *Inner Chapters,* 128).

reasoning, or cross-cultural dialogue. In the original Chinese text, the party that gives the illness or deformation to Ziyu is 造物者, that is, literally, the Creator. However, Legge translates it variously by employing not one but three terms: "Creator," "He," and "Heaven." "Creator" is closest in meaning to the original Chinese, but "Heaven" is also possible since the Chinese are familiar with this concept in Taoism. When used in such a context the word "He," however, clearly suggests, for Legge, a reflection upon the personal God of the Bible. However close Legge endeavors to remain to the original meaning of Chinese classical texts, his Christian missionary stance can never be entirely forgotten. The word "He" is, for him, suggestive of the God of the Bible, and reveals his tensions as a translator, both theologically and philosophically, with the culturally and religiously remote Taoism of Zhuangzi. In short, when Legge encounters the concept of determinism or fatalism in Taoism, he is left wondering if there is a God at all in Taoism. On the other hand, even though the deeply Christian Legge may not interpret each idea of Zhuangzi precisely, still his understanding of Taoism is remarkable and to the point. In his appraisal of the story of Ziyu Legge clearly recognized that such submission to one's lot is central to the teachings of Taoism.[7] Many years later Legge wrote with profound understanding of Taoism which, in his widely read book *The Religions of China* (1880), he described respectfully as "the name both of a religion and a philosophy."[8]

Besides Ziyu's story of being ill or deformed, there are other similar narratives in *Zhuangzi*. For example, in Book IV, which is called *Renjianshi* (that is, "The Way of the Human World"), there is a description of a character named Shu:

> There was the deformed object Shu. His chin seemed to hide his navel; his shoulders were higher than the crown of his head; the knot of his hair pointed to the sky; his five viscera were all compressed into the upper part of his body, and his two thigh bones were like ribs.[9]

Once again, although stricken with this terrible condition, Shu did not complain or question the way of the Creator. Indeed, when compared with Ziyu, Shu is even more optimistic. He could make a living for himself by

---

7. Zhuangzi, *Writings of Kwang-sze*, in Müller, *Sacred Books of the East*, 248.
8. Legge, *Religions of China*, 159.
9. Zhuangzi, *Writings of Kwang-sze*, 220. Here it can be seen that Legge's translation of "ulcer" in Book VI is problematic because the original words are the same in this passage. Word-for-word translation is impossible.

sharpening needles and washing clothes for others. He could support ten people by sifting rice and discarding the husks. Because of his condition he was free from conscription into the army. In the end, speaking on behalf of Shu, the author says that if a man who is crippled is able to support himself into good old age, then ordinary people with "crippled virtue" should achieve even more.

We can observe from what we have seen that when faced with terrible physical deformity or ailments, the general attitude in *Zhuangzi* is to submit to one's lot, to accept what you are given and to do what you can do. The reason or the cause of such ailments or deformity is never questioned. In other words, such characters never complain, doubt or question the Creator. It may then be suggested that this sense of passive-acceptance is one of the essential ideas in *Zhuangzi* and in Taoism.

What, then, of Job? A man also suffering deep afflictions through no fault of his own, Job is not satisfied or convinced about the reasons suggested by his "comforters" for the misfortunes that have happened to him. He refutes the charges laid upon him by his friends. Only after long questioning of the ways of God does Job come to acknowledge his own ignorance and inability, finally realizing that one cannot employ human conceptions of right and wrong to judge God. One can only learn to fear God, for his mystery lies beyond the boundary of human understanding. In the words of the literary critic Gabriel Josipovici:

> The book of Job is about the impossibility of man's ever understanding the causal links (the story), and yet his need to trust that God does indeed uphold the world, that there is a story there of which we are a part. It shows that man must neither simply accept that there is a story nor refuse to believe that there is one, but that it is his duty constantly to question God (and himself) about it.[10]

We see at once in the Old Testament story both the similarities with and the deep differences from the seemingly deterministic Taoism of *Zhuangzi*.

Zhuangzi

It is quite clear, on the other hand, that there are close literary similarities between the stories of *Zhuangzi* and the book of Job. Both are about good

---

10. Josipovici, *Book of God*, 290.

characters who suffer through no apparent fault of their own, and both have dialogues which reflect voices from different schools of thought. However, we should never forget that these two works grew from very different cultural origins. Zhuangzi offers his readers his conceptions of Taoism, which is one of the most important philosophical and religious schools of thoughts in ancient China. His writings, in short, are set within a specific historical and cultural context in ancient China.

As we have seen, there is a certain type of character who when stricken with illness or deformity thinks that submission to life and what it brings is what they should do without complaining and questioning. Besides the two examples already mentioned, there are other stories in *Zhuangzi* reflecting a similar attitude when, for example, people lose a spouse or a friend. Their characters are not only submissive but they even sing songs or manifest a certain happiness at funerals or other sad occasions.

In Book III ("The Way of Nourishing Life") of *Zhuangzi*, there is such a story. When Laodan (Laozi) dies, his friend Qinyi goes to his room to mourn, as is the custom. But Qinyi only utters three loud shouts and departs, and his disciples think that their master has not shown proper grief as a friend. Qinyi explains that "quiet acquiescence in what happens at its proper time, and quietly submitting (to its ceasing) afford no occasion for grief or for joy."[11] Such acquiescence is highly reminiscent of the ancient Christian teaching on *apatheia* or "dispassion," the refusal to be overwhelmed or displaced by strong emotions.[12] It is what the American Trappist monk Thomas Merton, in his study of the early Desert Fathers calls *quies*[13] (that is the fruit of purity of heart), and it is no accident that Merton was himself drawn to write upon *Zhuangzi* in his book *The Way of Chuang Tzu* (1965).

A similar disposition is found in the story of Zisanghu in Book VI of *Zhuangzi*. When Zisanghu dies and before he is buried, Confucius hears of this and sends his disciple Zigong to see if he can help or assist in any way. When Zigong arrives, someone is composing a song, and someone else is playing a lute. Zigong is very surprised and says that what they are doing is not appropriate for the occasion. But the two men simply look at each other and laugh out loud, saying that Zigong does not understand what is

11. Zhuangzi, *Writings of Kwang-sze*, in Müller, *Sacred Books of the East*, 199.

12. For a contemporary discussion of this in Christianity, see Williams, *Being Disciples*, 77–79.

13. Merton, *Wisdom*, 8.

appropriate. What these two mean is that dying is part of what the Creator has ordered. Therefore what we should do most appropriately is quietly accept and submit and even enjoy ourselves at the time of such a grievous incident.

The most familiar story of this sort is about Zhuangzi himself. It is narrated in Book XVIII ("Ultimate Happiness"). Zhuangzi's wife has died and his friend Huizi goes to give his condolences. When Huizi arrives he sees Zhuangzi sitting on the ground with his two legs straight in front of him, singing a song and banging on a pottery basin. Huizi chides Zhuangzi for his failure to grieve for his wife and even, apparently, to be enjoying himself. Zhuangzi replies that his wife has merely returned to the state in which she was before she was born and that now she is with nature once again. Nothing unnatural has taken place. Therefore, Zhuangzi concludes, why should he be sorrowful when his wife is lying between heaven and earth?

Why do these characters in *Zhuangzi* not question or complain about what has happened to them? Either they quietly accept and submit to their fate, or they seem to behave in extraordinary and surprising ways. But there is one occasion when Zhuangzi does question the ways of heaven. In the last passage of Book VI we find the story of Ziyu and Zisang, who were friends. It rains continuously for ten days and Ziyu fears that Zisang may be in distress. Ziyu wraps up some rice and goes to Ziyu's house to give it to him. When he comes near to Zisang's house, he hears from inside contradictory sounds of both singing and wailing. It is Zisang who is playing a lute and uttering the words "Father," "Mother," "Heaven," and "Men." Zisang is repeating these words over and over, singing and wailing all the time and so Ziyu goes into the house and inquires as to the cause of this behavior. Zisang replies (in Legge's translation):

> I was thinking, and thinking in vain, how it was that I was brought to such extremity. Would my parents have wished me to be so poor? Heaven overspreads all without any partial feeling, and so does Earth sustain all—would Heaven and Earth make me so poor with any unkindly feeling? I was trying to find out who had done it, and I could not do so. But here I am in this extremity!—it is what is appointed for me![14]

Legge significantly does not translate the original words of the last sentence literally. According to the original Chinese text, it is fate, lot or

---

14. Zhuangzi, *Writings of Kwang-sze*, in Müller, *Sacred Books of the East*, 258.

destiny (命) which made him so poor and be in such extremity. But who or what rules such fate or destiny, neither Zisang nor Zhuangzi himself asks further. Legge himself adds a significant footnote to this passage: "Here is the highest issue of Tàoism: unquestioning submission to what is beyond our knowledge and control."[15]

I suggest that here James Legge has misunderstood Zhuangzi's thought by confusing the thinking of Zhuangzi and that of Job. On the one hand I agree that it is true that the stories selected in Zhuangzi and Job have a surface similarity, but on the other hand they are quite different in their philosophical or theological significance. Here, Zhuangzi is showing his fatalist or determinist stance in which one does nothing, while Job is more about the act of faith in which he is not so much doing nothing but rather recognizing the power of God.

Historically and culturally, Chinese scholars of *Zhuangzi* through the ages, for example Qian Mu and Liu Xiaogan, have shown that peaceful acceptance and quiet submission to reality or fate is the central theme of this classical text.[16] Other scholars, such as Fang Yong, have also pointed out that it is not that Zhuangzi does not wish to ask about the way of heaven, but the context set within the stories gives him no choice.[17] This attitude of passive acceptance is the consequence of the apparent situation of helplessness or that of hopelessness. It is generally accepted that the first part of *Zhuangzi*, usually known as the "Internal Section" or "Inner Chapters," was probably written by Zhuangzi himself, and the other two parts, called the "External Section" and the "Miscellaneous Section," were written later or collected by his disciples and their disciples after them. The theme and ideas established by Zhuangzi in the Internal Section are expressive of the essential spirit of the whole book. Zhuangzi himself lived in the period of the Warring States (403–221 BCE), a time of turbulence and poverty in China.[18] In these violent days, Zhuangzi lived in poverty, but he "despised wealth and rank, power and fame, endeavoring to keep independent individuality

---

15. Zhuangzi, *Writings of Kwang-sze*, in Müller, *Sacred Books of the East*, 258.

16. Qian Mu, *Collection of Annotations of Zhuangzi*; Xiaogan, *Philosophy of Zhuangzi*. Qian Mu moved to Hong Kong and Taiwan after the political change in mainland China in the 1950s but continued to represent traditional Chinese culture. Liu Xiao-gan was representative of the first generation to study Zhuangzi after the reform and opening up in mainland China in the 1980s.

17. Zhuangzi, *Zhuangzi* [Fang Yong].

18. See Ebrey, *Cambridge Illustrated History of China*, 38–43.

in troubled times and seeking for an unfettered and unrestrained spirit."[19] Zhuangzi's attitude of passive acceptance and submission reflected in his stories of suffering and deprivation should be contextualized in a period in China that was devastated by war and was rife with political conspiracy and deception. In this season of darkness "innocent people were slayed without reason and society became a trap where human beings became brutalized." The social context of Zhuangzi's time can be described as "a period of history where blood was on the rampage and which mercilessly revealed itself before Zhuangzi." In this winter of despair Zhuangzi reveals an evil and vicious human world in which the Taoist "passive attitude and way of dealing with oneself and with others are a reflection of helplessness."[20]

Philosophically, this teaching of Zhuangzi was later developed and called "doing nothing" (无 为) and it forms one of the central concepts in Taoism. It has recently been the subject of studies of contemporary culture in such writings as Wang Hai's 2016 essay "The Power of Powerlessness," linking "doing nothing" or *wu wei* with the thought of the French philosopher Maurice Blanchot.[21] As discussed above, in most cases these deprived individuals do not question who or which party consigns them to such a miserable state, with the only exception of Zisang's case, when he exclaims that it is fate, lot or destiny that makes him become what he is. Then what is exactly the nature of this fate, lot or destiny in Zhuangzi's Taoism, and what is its relationship with the supreme Dao?

In *Zhuangzi*, there are a number of places where Zhuangzi writes about fate. For instance, in Book V ("Dechongfu"), Zhuangzi illustrated this idea of fate through the speaking of Confucius: "Death and life, perseveration and ruin, failure and success, poverty and wealth, superiority and inferiority, blame and praise, hunger and thirst, cold and hot—these are the changes of circumstances, the operation of our appointed lot."[22] Although Zhuangzi is considered to have been the original follower of Laozi in Taoism, this concept of our "appointed lot" is actually drawn from Confucius. In Book XII of the *Analects*, Zixia, one of Confucius's disciples, says: "There is the following saying which I have heard, Death and life have their

---

19. Yuan Xingpei, *History of Chinese Literature* [text slightly edited].

20. Chen Guying, *Contemporary Annotation and Translation of Zhuangzi*, 127 [text slightly edited].

21. Wang Hai, "Power of Powerlessness: Rediscovering the Radicality of Wu Wei in Daoism through Blanchot," in Jasper, *Poetics*, 195–204.

22. Zhuangzi, *Writings of Kwang-sze*, in Müller, *Sacred Books of the East*, 231.

determined appointment; riches and honours depend upon Heaven."²³ Here James Legge rendered the idea of "lot" as "determined appointment," which is not an exact interpretation. Another British sinologist Arthur Waley rendered "lot" as heaven ("Death and life are the decree of Heaven; wealth and rank depend upon the will of Heaven"²⁴), which is more accurate since in ancient Chinese culture, whether in Confucianism or in Taoism, of these two Chinese characters 命 literally means "lot" and 天 literally means "heaven." They are equal in meaning and usage on some occasions and are often used together as one phrase. Thus it is reasonable to conclude that in these deprivation stories the party that establishes these extreme situations is *fate* or heaven. However, Zhuangzi seems to expand the Confucian idea of "fate" or "heaven" by including not only the question of death and life, wealth and rank, but also that of superiority and inferiority, blame and praise, etc.

Although Zhuangzi developed the idea of "fate" from Confucianism, his idea of "heaven" is evolved from Laozi. It seems that in the *Daodejing*, heaven is in such a superior position that sometimes it is equal to Dao itself (e.g., chapters 16 and 47). It is often the case that Laozi's heaven is used in parallel to earth (e.g., chapter 5: "Heaven and Earth are ruthless"; chapter 7: "Heaven is eternal, the Earth everlasting"; chapter 25: "Something formless yet complete . . . existed before heaven and earth"²⁵). Thus the heaven of the *Daodejing* is more inclined to be in a materialized form. However, the heaven in *Zhuangzi* is often used in parallel to human beings or human actions, thus being more formless and unspeakable. By discussing "lot" and "heaven," we come to the key concept in Taoism—*Dao*, or "the Way." In the *Daodejing*, heaven is often set in parallel to, or even equal to, *Dao*, which is more inclined to be in form, like heaven. Whereas in *Zhuangzi*, *Dao* is seldom mentioned and when it is it is more likely to be formless, being immaterial and unspeakable. In the *Daodejing*, Dao is called the beginning and linked to "to have" and "to have not" (at the very beginning of the *Daodejing*, it says that the *Dao* is both nameless and named at the same time, the former being the beginning of heaven and earth and the latter being the mother of all things), whereas in *Zhuangzi*, Zhuangzi himself explained his doubt: if there is this beginning in Laozi's sense, is there a

---

23. Confucius, *Analects*, 252–53.
24. Confucius, *Analects*, 147.
25. Lao Tzu, *Tao Te Ching*, 11, 15, 53.

beginning in the beginning?[26] By questioning in this way, Zhuangzi made his special contribution in the development of Taoism by transforming the quite materialized *Dao* into a more formless one, thus developing Laozi's philosophical Dao into a philosophical, literary and ritual *Dao*. Perhaps we, as readers, can imitate Zhuangzi's particular approach and ask this question: As far as *Dao* is concerned, is there a "bereshith" in the "bereshith," if there is a "bereshith?"

After discussing the historical, cultural and philosophical significance of the deprivation stories in *Zhuangzi*, we may look at them from another perspective, that is, the dialogical principles of Bakhtin. If we put the context in which *Zhuangzi* was written and place it in a larger dimension, we may find that Zhuangzi's attitude, whether it be termed as passive acceptance or "doing nothing," is only one school of thought in that epoch of tremendous change in Chinese thought and religion. The traditional Chinese four-character phrase "One-hundred School Contending in Thoughts" (百家争鸣) is a vivid description of the emergence and development of different schools of thought in the Spring and Autumn period (722–481 BCE) and Warring States times in China. Zhuangzi's Taoism was not only one of the outstanding schools of thought in these early periods in Chinese history, but was also both influencing and being influenced by other schools. For instance, as discussed above, in *Zhuangzi* there are a number of passages about Confucius such as in Zisang's story. There are also passages about Laozi. Confucian voices and Taoist voices, even two different voices in the same Taoist school, are contending, questioning, and influencing each other, generating creativity in that time. In his influential book *The Origin and Goal of History* (1949), the German-Swiss philosopher Karl Jaspers argued that in this Spring and Autumn and Warring States period, two of the three major religions in China (Confucianism, Taoism, and Buddhism) were born and then institutionalized. Philosophers and writers such as Confucius, Laozi, Zhuangzi, and Mo-zi form a special part of what Jaspers called the Axial Age, along with more or less contemporary philosophical thinkers in India and in the West such as Socrates and Plato. Jaspers further pointed out that cultures in the Axial Age such as those of ancient Greece, the Hebrew peoples, China and India went through a transformative stage. That is, they all transcended their predecessors in the so-called primitive cultures. Those ancient cultures such as those of ancient

---

26. Bo, *Philosophy of Zhuangzi*, 156.

Babylon and Egypt, which did not go through the same process, died and became cultural fossils.[27]

Jaspers also suggests that some classic texts in both the East and the West were formed in similar epochs and even in the same age. That is the case, he would argue, for *Zhuangzi* and the book of Job. As we have seen the concept of "doing nothing" is at the heart of Zhuangzi's Taoism. However, the fundamental concept in the book of Job is different. Although there are clear similarities such as the plot of stories, the literary narration and the dialogues, there is nothing like "doing nothing" in the book of Job and here the Hebraic and the Chinese are clearly distinct.

The Book of Job

Fundamentally the book of Job is a theological text, a poetic reflection on theodicy: how can the good and loving God allow innocent people to suffer? With its ancient origins in very early Egyptian, Babylonian and Sumerian texts,[28] the theme of Job continues in poetry and philosophy, the greatest example in English literature being John Milton's *Paradise Lost* (1667).

The book of Job actively seeks to justify the ways of God to men. Job does not "do nothing" but rather strives to develop his own theology. Briefly here we need to establish something of the historical and cultural background of the text. Scholars generally agree that Job is to be understood as a just man living approximately in the time of the Jewish patriarch Abraham though not himself a Hebrew.[29] The story of Job extends back deep into oral traditions and it was long thought that the book of Job was written down in the reign of Solomon. Tradition has even attributed the book to Solomon himself.[30] More recent studies reveal that the book was most probably written, or, more accurately, compiled, in the Hellenistic Age or at the time of the Babylonian Exile (ca. 597–539 BCE). It has even been suggested that the book of Job was first written as a verse play as during the Hellenistic period there were many newly built theatres in the region of Palestine.[31] Others would argue that the time of writing or

---

27. For further comment on China and the Axial Age, see Ziolkowski, "Axial Age," 129–50; Bellah, *Religion in Human Evolution*, 399–480.
28. See Snaith, *Book of Job*.
29. See further Crenshaw, "Job," 331–34.
30. See Young, *Introduction to the Old Testament*, 355; *Chinese Study Bible*, 769.
31. Weizhi, *Twelve Lectures*, 307.

compilation was the period of the Babylonian Exile or shortly after it when the Jewish people, under oppressive conditions, were facing a crisis and a profound challenge to their religious faith and national culture.[32] This later dating makes sense inasmuch as the questioning spirit in the book of Job is quite different from other early Pentateuchal stories such as the testing of Abraham. In Genesis 22, it seems, Abraham never doubted the astounding order given by God and there is no description of Abraham's psychological state when faced with losing his only son at such an old age.[33] However, Job ponders intensely upon what has brought all his woes upon him since he has kept to the ways of God so piously. He questions what justification there is for what has happened to him and such questioning or inquiry, whatever its ancient roots, is also one of the most prominent features of Greek philosophy. At the same time Job's questioning of heaven's justice may be taken in the context of what the Jewish people themselves were suffering in the exilic and post-exilic period. The people who once, as they thought, complied with God's covenant so faithfully, who respected its laws and who were chosen and protected by Jehovah, had now lost their homeland and were governed by alien nations. They were confronted with the inevitable question: why has Jehovah deserted them when they were so faithful? The question is that of Job.

Here it should be mentioned that in both *Zhuangzi* and Job the characters do not question the way of heaven (although in the beginning Job does question the justification for a good man to be punished while ultimately he does not question the way of God). However, their philosophical and religious differences are quite obvious and deserve more attention than they have been given. Zhuangzi's not questioning heaven is a reflection of determinist or fatalist conception in Taoism while Job's not questioning God is a reflection of the fact that, ultimately Job is a man of faith.

Against the background of Mikhail Bakhtin's theory of discourse both active and passive,[34] Job can be considered as the "active" narrator or learned interpreter who is deeply concerned about the Jewish people's fate and is eagerly seeking a way out of bondage. Job's three "comforters" represent a more "passive" traditional Hebrew religious culture, insisting on a pattern of cause and effect. If we suffer ills there must be a reason for it.

---

32. Crenshaw, "Job," 332.

33. See Auberbach's classic essay "Odysseus's Scar," which describes Genesis 22 as "fraught with background."

34. See Todorov, *Mikhail Bakhtin*, 70–72.

It is generally agreed that the passages concerning Elihu were inserted later into the text and that Elihu himself is probably Jewish.[35] It might be suggested that the Elihu passages are relatively insignificant because Job does not respond to him at all and if these passages are omitted the narrative line between Job's talking and God's responding out of the storm would not be disturbed. On the other hand it could equally be argued that Elihu's contribution is as important as other discussions in the book of Job if we place the whole text into the later context of the Hellenistic Age or the Babylonian Exile. Elihu can then be considered as a representative of Hellenistic Jews who held views that were markedly different from more traditional perspectives, but at the same time who were, perhaps, not insightful or learned enough to seek out an appropriate theological solution. God, after all, does not respond to Elihu but only to the more profound Job directly. Job stands distinctly apart from his three friends, against whom God is directly angry (Job 42:7), and Elihu.

Conclusion

When proclaiming James Legge's contribution to the bridging of intercultural communication between China and the West, it is also important to recognize that he was probably confusing the philosophy of Zhuangzi and the theology of Job. My aim has been to separate and point out the differences between the two traditions. "Doing nothing" is an attitude of escaping from troublesome and war-fraught times, which has its profound influence in Chinese culture in almost every aspect. The book of Job, the story of which appears much earlier than the compilation of the Bible itself, shows Job's staunch faith in God in troubled times for the Jewish people.

To some extent, Zhuangzi's ideas are close to Stoic thinking, though there are also crucial differences. The implication of much thinking about comparative religion and culture in the nineteenth century, following such pivotal works as Sir Edward Tylor's *Researches into the Early History of Mankind* (1865),[36] was that all religions have a common origin. But, to be fair to him, after his many years as a Western scholar and missionary in China, this was not a model to which James Legge subscribed. In *The Religions of China*, a mature book published at the end of his life, Legge is quite clear

---

35. See *Chinese Study Bible*, 800.
36. See further James, *Comparative Religion*, 15–34.

that cultures and religions, even when they have profound similarities, have even more profound differences.

For *Zhuangzi* and the book of Job, the literary similarities in narration and character are clear and important, but we should not underestimate their cultural and philosophical differences. In his great translation of the Taoist classic, which he renders as the *Tâo Teh King*, Legge readily admits the impossibility of translating *Tao*. He simply leaves it as transliterated, noting its similarity with another untranslatable term from the Greek, the *Logos* of the first chapter of St. John's Gospel.[37] To Legge, as a Christian, *Tao* is the *equivalent* of something like "duty to God"—but he is not prepared to go further than this, and he quotes his great predecessor in Chinese studies in Paris, M. Abel Rémusat, writing in 1823: "Ce mot me semble ne pas pouvoir être bien traduit, si ce n'est pas le mot λογος dans le triple sens de souverain Être, de raison, et de parole."[38] (This word seems to me to be not properly translatable, unless as the word λογος in the threefold sense of sovereign Being, reason, and word.)

The similarities between *Zhuangzi* and the book of Job are mainly in their textual or narrative appearance, or we might say that they only share literary similarities. But as far as culture is concerned they are different, one being essentially a philosophical and literary text, passive in its nature, and the other more profoundly and actively theological. However, although we cannot be naïve to the differences between these classical texts in different cultures, it is possible today that we share through them a dialogical spirit such as the hospitality of Scriptural Reasoning suggests. Classical or scriptural texts remain, in a sense, timeless, their terms synchronic across all cultural and religious barriers. In this spirit, both of our texts, Chinese and biblical writings, continue to speak to us, bound together by their common literary qualities and characteristics. In them, literature becomes a binding force across religious and philosophical differences. With a willingness to have dialogue about such texts, differences can be tolerated or reassessed and articulated. Thus the literary qualities of *Zhuangzi* and the book of Job bind them together even as we address their profound religious differences.

---

37. Müller, *Sacred Books of the East*, 12–13, 47.

38. Rémusat, quoted in James Legge, "Introduction to *The Texts of Tâoism*," in Müller, *Sacred Books of the East*, 12.

2

The Book of Job and *Zhuangzi*
A Response

DAVID JASPER

WHILE THE SCHOLARSHIP OF intercultural studies is at pains to describe and point out the differences between the ideas of Zhuangzi and the book of Job, what strikes me more forcibly, and increasingly so, are the similarities between them as products of Karl Jaspers's admittedly debated Axial Age as presented in *The Origin and Goal of History*, and never more so than in their indomitable sense of the human capacity for endurance and stoically accepting all that life can throw at us by way of undeserved suffering and misery.

We know from the Psalms that the ancient Hebrews were wont to reflect on the apparent injustice of the wicked person who seems to flourish and the good person who gains nothing for his goodness beyond poverty, suffering and humiliation. Jesus's great parable of Dives and Lazarus (Luke 16:19–31) seems to offer some assurance that fortunes may be reversed in the world to come, justice seen to be done, but both *Zhuangzi* and the book of Job are firmly fixed in the often miserable conditions of this life and the capacity of human beings to endure sufferings that are somehow, for no apparent reason, thrust upon them. I have never been satisfied with Jung's description of Job at the beginning of his book *Answer to Job* (1952):

> What else could a half-crushed human worm, groveling in the dust, reasonably answer in the circumstances? In spite of his pitiable littleness and feebleness, this man knows that he is confronted with a superhuman being who is personally most easily provoked. He also knows that it is far better to withhold all moral reflections, to say nothing of certain moral demands which ought, after all, to apply to a god.[1]

Apart from the fact that this seems to miss the point entirely on the matter of "moral reflections" in the book of Job (failing to move on from the immature cry that "things are not fair"), it also belittles the human dignity that Job sustains in spite of all. Job is no "half-crushed human worm, groveling in the dust." He is closer to being the prototype of the tragic hero, dignified in his misery.

What strikes me most forcibly in Guang-an's dialogical review of *Zhuangzi* and the book of Job are the ultimately quite different foundations upon which they build their sense of what it is to be human. The Taoist concept of *wu wei*[2] which we can roughly translate as "doing nothing" is very far from being a kind of passive acceptance, a *failure* to do anything in the face of overwhelming odds. Rather, as one recent western commentator has suggested, "the true meaning of the term *wu wei* is something like 'not doing anything against the flow' or 'not doing anything that does not have its roots in Tao.'"[3] The Taoist concept of universal *harmony* and balance is very different from the utterly theocentric and contradictory world of the book of Job.

This ancient text of the Hebrew Bible is founded upon a sense of *story*. As Guang-an's quotation from Gabriel Josipovici's *The Book of God* (1988) suggests, there is a story inherent in God's upholding of the world, and we are a part of that story without being able finally to understand it as a complete whole. We are in the midst, perplexed and confused. We are caught, then, in the situation of believing that there is a story and yet constantly finding ourselves being called upon to question its author and our part in it. That, perhaps, is why the book of Job has repeatedly attracted the attention of novelists and story-tellers from the writers of the Talmud to Herman Melville and the contemporary Scottish novelist Muriel Spark. Spark's wonderful novel on Job (which is also a retelling of the Job story), *The Only*

---

1. Jung, *Answer to Job*, 7–8.
2. See also on *Tess of the D'Urbervilles* and the question of fate below, 34–55.
3. Towler, "Introduction," xvi.

Problem (1984), has its roots in her earliest writings and preoccupations. Spark's first novel, *The Comforters* (1957) takes its name from Job's so-called "comforters" and is a story about a woman who becomes aware that she is a character in a novel (as indeed she is), despite the efforts of her "comforters" to persuade her otherwise. Like the book of Job this is a text the texture of which is self-aware, to an extent, for just as the reader knows that Job is the subject of a divine experiment, so Job himself clearly has a sense of this also, despite the efforts of *his* comforters to argue otherwise.[4] He is part of a greater story, a character who will not be told what to do. The biblical critic Hugh Pyper continues:

> [Job] is aware of an "author" in his life. Spark and Job raise the huge question of the freedom of the character and the author. On the face of it, the character is entirely at the author's mercy. However, authors can also find that the character takes over and demands that the plot follow a particular course.[5]

Literature is here taking us to the very heart of Christian theology as it struggles with the ineluctable fate that is Job's lot, yet also his capacity to challenge and defy that fate. Job does not suffer his fate gladly, at least in the first instance. At the same time the book of Job is perhaps the earliest and still one of the greatest works in the western tradition to confront the matter of unmerited human suffering and the refusal to subscribe to the obvious naivety of the simple moral equation that we suffer because we have deserved it. Behave well and you will be rewarded. But the psalmist knows that this is not so. What is the God of love doing when good people suffer?

> Why, O lord, do you stand far off?
> Why do you hide yourself in times of trouble?
> In arrogance the wicked persecute the poor (Ps 10:1–2 NRSV)

In the book of Job, as in Psalm 10 (at least until verse 12), there is an edginess, almost a petulance with the God who is yet at the heart of all things. Such petulance extends also to the reader. As Hugh Pyper expresses it: "So the discomfort that the text causes the reader by its seeming incoherence is part of its status as a poem."[6] The point of course is that we human beings never know the whole story in which we live and have our being, though we may decide to live by faith that the whole story does finally

---

4. I am indebted here to Pyper, "Reader in Pain."
5. Pyper, "Reader in Pain," 234.
6. Pyper, "Reader in Pain," 242.

exist and that all shall be well in spite of everything being apparently to the contrary.

The book of Job, I have always thought, ends with its tongue firmly in its cheek. God gives up his persecution of Job and heaps huge, indeed ridiculous, rewards upon him. His family joins in the general celebration. After all—all's well that ends well. "They showed him sympathy and comforted him for all the evil that the Lord had brought upon him; and each of them gave him a piece of money and a gold ring" (Job 42:11 NRSV). They are like loving parents who give their child a reward for being so brave at the dentist's. After all, as Harvey Gotham, the protagonist of Spark's novel *The Only Problem* not unreasonably suggested, "God is a shit" in his treatment of the good man Job.[7] But then, as Harvey is quick to point out to his outraged Auntie Pet, he is making here a literary observation. Of course he is not talking blasphemously about God our creator, but "a fictional character in the *Book of Job*, called God."[8] Well, yes, but God is only God in story, and *The Only Problem* ends, like all good stories, with a fictional domestic paradise. All writers know (as Dostoevsky and Wittgenstein teach us, among a thousand others) that even as every author finishes one book, and ends one story, he or she is already moving on to the next—the narrative that always eludes us. Harvey Gotham is asked what he is going to do now that he has finished his book on Job. His answer is unconvincing: "Live another hundred and forty years. I'll have three daughters, Clara, Jemima and Eye-Paint."[9] As we say with some cynicism in Scotland, "Aye, right."

But that, of course, does not answer the question. As Josipovici nicely put it:

> Muriel Spark has understood that the end of Job, like the beginning, is not a mere frame. It is the assertion of the fact that meaning will never be able to catch up with life.[10]

This seems to me to be utterly un-Chinese. The Taoist is not concerned with wrestling with the text of the story that ends only in the world to come, if it ends at all, and in the mystery of God, who in spite of all we continue to believe somehow loves us.

---

7. Spark, *Only Problem*, 123.
8. Spark, *Only Problem*, 135.
9. Spark, *Only Problem*, 189.
10. Josipovici, *Book of God*, 290.

But I see Guang-an, who is my friend, looking over my shoulder, smiling and shaking his head. For our similarities are, in the end, greater than our differences.

4

A Textual and Cross-Cultural Investigation of "Fate" in Thomas Hardy's *Tess of the D'Urbervilles*

Ou Guang-an

AT THE CONCLUSION OF Thomas Hardy's novel *Tess of the D'Urbervilles* (1891), the tragic life of the protagonist comes to an end because "the President of the Immortals," Hardy's literal translation of two ancient Greek words in *Prometheus Bound*, a Greek tragedy assumed to be written by Aeschylus, "has ended his sport with Tess."[1] After such a long sorrowful journey of following the twists and turns of Tess's life the reader, whose attention is brought nearly to the edge of breaking down in the face of Tess's tragedy, is over-sensitive to the word "sport," with its ironic implication. One of the primary meanings of the word "sport," according to the *Shorter Oxford English Dictionary*, is "pastime afforded by the endeavour to take or kill wild animals, game or fish," with the extended sense of "amusement, jest, mirth or merriment."[2] If we follow the explanation strictly, Tess is just like game, a fish, or a wild animal that lives merely to be "killed" or "played with." Then the critical question arises naturally: *who* is killing or playing Tess as a sport? Is it a religious deity, society with its class or prejudices, or simply the "President of Immortals"? After reading the novel in English and in its three popular Chinese translations (three is only a small number

---

1. Hardy, *Tess of the D'Urbervilles* [Elledge], 330.
2. *Shorter Oxford English Dictionary*, 1980.

of the Chinese translations of the book available), as a Chinese scholar who has been reading works of Confucius from a very early age and then Taoist thought some years later, I cannot but help thinking that it is "fate," the unknown pre-primeval force, that is playing with the poor soul, when all ancient, medieval and modern conceptions or mechanisms, especially the consolations of religion and the safeguards of society, fail to rescue Tess, a "pure woman," as a human being.

However, my other identity as an English language learner for twenty-six years[3] and an English language and literature teacher in China for fifteen years would make me readily link the idea of "fate" in Hardy's novel to that of ancient Greek culture, especially with its tragedies and mythological figures. At first sight, there are clearly some similarities between the two, whereas a further close reading would demonstrate the differences also. For Tess's fate is inevitably entangled with the practice of the Christian religion in late Victorian English society, its social rules or laws, its class financial systems

With the lack of any form of salvation, either religious or secular, to redeem Tess, and with the mocking "sport of the President of Immortals," Tess's tragic ending seems to reflect a prevailing pessimism in Hardy's later novels in which one can do nothing, in the novelist's own words, about "the tragical conditions of life." This concept of "doing nothing" in Hardy's writing rings a familiar bell in the ears of a Chinese reader because, as I have shown already in the previous chapter, that is also close to the quintessence of Taoism, a system of thought equally important as Confucianism in Chinese culture. A detailed investigation of the idea of "fate" both in Confucianism and Taoism and a comparison between them and the sense of fate in *Tess of the D'Urbervilles* would reveal unique insights into the differences between Chinese culture and nineteenth-century British culture as well as their similarities, thus making cross-cultural communication possible and desirable.

---

3. English has been a compulsory course in the primary and secondary school curriculum in China since the 1980s. It usually starts in the first year in junior middle school, that is, at the average age of twelve for students. This is often the case in country schools, while in cities it could start as early as the third year in primary school (normally eight years old for children) or even as early as the first year (six years of age).

Failure of Religion and Society in Tess's Salvation

It is perhaps safe to say that religious elements and social factors are the two major forces causing the doom of Tess, and her eventual death at the rope's end. As for the former, Hardy seems to demonstrate a rather contradictory attitude toward Christianity, with his merciless accusation of the Church and Christianity on one hand and his frequent quotation from and allusion to the biblical texts and their extension on the other. The implication might also be that the Christian religion is engaged in a kind of "sport" with Tess. There seems to be no hint of possible salvation either from the Church or its ministers.

Being an English professor in a Chinese university who teaches English major students about English language and literature, there is an accumulated perception on my part about the importance of culture in the history of English literature. Over the years I have developed a sense that the Greco-Roman, or, more precisely the Hellenic tradition, and the Hebrew tradition from which, through the Bible, Christianity largely emerges, are the two essential sources of European culture, English culture included.[4] In W. B. Yeats's "vision" of the cycles of history the Greek classic tradition is the backbone of the two millennia before Christ with its possible origin in "a sudden blow" in the poem "Leda and the Swan," and Christianity holds the center of the two thousand years after Christ with "some revelation . . . at hand," or the *parousia* when these two thousand years are approaching their end.[5] With my preliminary and even superficial understanding of Christianity, it seems clear that it is at the very heart of western culture and history, and this is still the case in the late Victorian England of Hardy's novel, even though the history of that time was already beginning to witness its decline. However, as can be easily seen in *Tess*, not only is salvation out of the question, but also it is the very behavior of people or parties related to the Church that constitute at least some of the destructive forces that lead to Tess's tragedy in the end.

Anyone who has read something about Christianity would quickly recognize the meaning of the word "angel," which is generally linked with blessing, good news or even salvation. However, the character of Angel Clare in the novel does not fulfill that expectation. After Tess confesses to

---

4. It is interesting to note that in Chinese these two traditions are called 两希文明 (notice the same first word 希 xi in both names) with the first being translated as 希腊文明 and the latter as 希伯来文明.

5. Yeats, *Poems*, 260, 235.

Angel about her past, his reaction seems to be that of a totally different man to the Angel who had professed his love for her:

> His face had withered. In the strenuousness of his concentration he treadled fitfully on the floor. . . . He looked vacantly at her, to resume with dazed senses. . . . These and other of his words were nothing but the perfunctory babble of the surface while the depths remain paralyzed.[6]

Seeing Angel's reaction to her confession, a heart-broken Tess implores him to forgive her in the name of their love, showing how desperate she is when the moment she is afraid of most finally arrives. Angel answers Tess's imploring by saying that the woman he loved is simply "another woman" in her shape and that he considers Tess's action as "prestidigitation," a word which would surely rouse the reader's curiosity, as to how he could think of such a formal word in such an agitated situation. The important thing to notice here is that when Angel is uttering this word he is saying it with the words "my God," seeming to suggest he is looking for some sort of divine power to sustain him through the agony, however far he is diverting from the direction his clergyman father would like him to take. With this "power" he also readily admits that Tess was, like King Lear "more sinned against than sinning."[7] But even with this admission, he would not forgive Tess because in his eyes she is another woman now, not unstained but an "impure" woman, whose sin has been forced upon her. The salvation-bringing "angel" fails to rescue Tess in an utterly ironic way.

What deserves further attention here is Angel's "justification" of his action by quoting social criteria and laws after failing to find justifiable excuses in the Christian situation. Of such things, it seems to him, Tess is simply ignorant.

> Don't, Tess; don't argue. Different societies, different manners. You almost make me say you are an unapprehending peasant woman, who have never been initiated into the proportions of social things.

---

6. Hardy, *Tess (Library Edition)*, 291–92.

7. When discussing the "purity" or "impurity" of Tess, one scholar points out that Tess is "an almost standard woman" by stating that it is "the patriarchal hegemony within which she is constructed" that "silences Tess" (Tess's death at the end and no confession from her before that). See Goode, *Thomas Hardy*, 124.

> O Tess—you are too, too—childish—unformed—crude, I suppose! I don't know what you are. You don't understand the law—you don't understand![8]

Besides this, there is another factor that influences Angel's failing to forgive Tess. It is his intellectual and "logical" rigidity:

> Within the remote depths of his constitution, so gentle and affectionate as he was in general, there lay hidden a hard logical deposit, like a vein of metal in a soft loam, which turned the edge of everything that attempted to traverse it. It had blocked his acceptance of the Church; it blocked his acceptance of Tess.[9]

Even though Angel does change his attitude after his experience in Brazil (an extraordinary experience deserving critical attention in any discussion about the historical placing of the novel in the nineteenth century, and a necessary one for the plot's development), the scene that describes Tess's confession and Angel's refusal to forgive is the climax of the novel, the summit of the narration, and the most significant event that lays the foundation of the tragic tone in the whole story. Thus the salvation-bringing Angel is truly a "misnamed Angel."

Besides her possible salvation through Angel Clare, there are two other episodes in the novel that are the critical moments when Tess could be "saved" both in a religious and in a secular sense. One is Tess's pleading to the clergyman for a Christian burial for her child and the other is Angel's two brothers' action when Tess is helpless and seeks to find Angel at his parent's home. Tess's musing on the christening of her baby and on the securing of a Christian burial for the child could only be answered by the parson of the parish because only through the church is this "doctrinally sufficient." And the answer is a negative from the vicar, though how he "reconciled his answer with the strict notions he supposed himself to hold on these subjects it is beyond a layman's power to tell," even though for a short moment he is moved by Tess's "dignity" and "the strange tenderness in her voice."[10] In him the "man" and the "ecclesiastic" are at odds with one another. On her way to Angel's family home, Tess's expectation of some comforting news from Angel's family is "crushed" by her accidentally overhearing harsh comments from Angel's two brothers, one regretting Angel's

---

8. Thomas Hardy, *Tess (Library Edition)*, 297, 305.
9. Thomas Hardy, *Tess (Library Edition)*, 308.
10. Thomas Hardy, *Tess (Library Edition)*, 121–22.

"precipitancy in throwing himself away upon a dairy-maid" and the other saying Angel's marriage is an "ill-considered" one which "seems to have completed that estrangement." With these words and comments comes the crucial incident of these two brothers, sons of the church, finding and deciding the fate of Tess's pair of boots which were bought by Angel. Tess's original intention had been to hide and to "save" them after wearing them over the "roughest part of the road." Ironically they not only do not know who the boots belong to but also it is decided to "carry them home for some poor person," which reveals the crucial question: who is, indeed, the person that really needs to be cared for?

Besides religion's "sporting" with Tess, which is at the very heart of Tess's tragic ending, another agency that "sports" with Tess's life is the society of Victorian England with its "responsibilities," its customs, laws, and regulations, bringing Tess to her inevitable doom.

First it is her sense of responsibility to her own poor family that initiates Tess's seemingly inevitable step by step decline. Being the eldest daughter, Tess has to shoulder the responsibility of supporting her family when her parents refuse to undertake the task that should be theirs, both of them being immersed in the fantasy of owning an extinct family name with the ludicrous belief that it would bring them material and social betterment. When their horse Prince, the backbone of the family income, dies accidently, led by the obligation of taking responsibility for the family, Tess, an innocent and uneducated girl of seventeen, goes to their *nouveau riche* "relative's" house to work where she walks into the trap of the villainous Alec d'Urberville. When the family loses the favor of Alec because Tess refuses to be taken as his mistress after she has buried her child, it is her sense of responsibility again, as well as the desire to escape, that pushes Tess to find another life in the Valley of the Great Dairies.

Waking from the seemingly endless pain of Angel's desertion of her and reminded by her accompanying dairy maids that she actually holds the responsibilities of wife to Angel and of daughter-in-law to Angel's parents, Tess goes to Angel's parental home, his father's rectory, only to have her heart broken again by Angel's brothers' harsh words and their merciless behavior concerning her old boots. When all seems to be hopeless in her own family, with the family house taken over by the landlord and the family cheated out of another possible rented house, Tess, with her almost unbearable responsibility for the survival of her family, finally becomes the mistress of Alec d'Urberville at The Herons, "a stylish lodging-house" in the fashionable town of Sandbourne. And finally, with the law bearing down upon her as a murderer and when Tess knows that there is no escape from the inevitable outcome, out of responsibility for her family again, she asks Angel to "watch over 'Liza-Lu, train her and teach her and bring her up" because Tess knows clearly this younger sister of hers would be the breadwinner of the family when she dies. Thus the responsibility of supporting the family passes on from the eldest daughter, the final scene with Angel and 'Liza-Lu deliberately echoing the end of *Paradise Lost* as the man and the woman set out into the harsh and fallen world.

"Responsibility" is one of the social standards that regulate people's lives in a religious country. Besides that there are other social standards that are "killing" and "playing" with Tess to her tragic end. It is her beauty that earns Tess the jealousy of her fellow working girls, with the typical example of Tess's almost getting into a fight with the "dark queen" when the latter's treacle is running from the basket on her head, "descending to some distance below her waist, like a Chinaman's queue."[11] Because of this jealousy Tess is forced to jump on the back of the horse Alec is riding, which inevitably adds to the impression that she is more favored by the master of the house and pushes Tess a step further in her disastrous entanglement with Alec. When Tess's child Sorrow dies, the narration is tear-provoking and anger-provoking at the same time:

> So passed away Sorrow the Undesired—that intrusive creature, that bastard gift of shameless Nature who respects not the social law; a waif to whom eternal Time had been a matter of days merely, who knew not that such things as years and centuries ever were; to whom the cottage interior was the universe, the week's weather

---

11. Thomas Hardy, *Tess (Library Edition)*, 81. Here is the only place in the novel that Hardy mentions China or any other Oriental region. The queue hanging on the back of the head could be identified as the typical and most easily-recognizable image of a Chinese man since the latter half of nineteenth century to the first half of twentieth century. This stereotype and the use of the term "Chinaman" are quite possibly the limits of Hardy's knowledge of China, and this forms a remarkable contrast between Hardy and other contemporary writers such as William Butler Yeats or David Herbert Lawrence. Indeed although Hardy was a voracious reader, his reading and experience outside Dorset seems not to have included information about China or other Oriental countries. It would seem that Hardy was rather sensitive to the fact that he did not receive much of a formal education, such as going to university. Ironically, he was to receive a number of honorary degrees from universities as his fame as a writer spread.

climate, new-born babyhood human existence, and the instinct to suck human knowledge.[12]

It is tear-provoking because one cannot but feel anything except the deepest sympathy for the innocent child who was brought to this world without knowing anything, and anger-provoking because such an innocent child has to be named as Sorrow and be considered as "undesired," "intrusive" even to the point of the notorious word "bastard," nothing but a kind of "offense against society." All of these things point to that ultimate factor which works against Tess and her child—social law. When religious elements fail in the possible salvation of Tess and the preservation of her child, social law also prevents their salvation and preservation in a similarly cruel way. Angel himself claims it will be recalled, that there are "different manners in different societies" and repeatedly says, with heavy irony, that Tess is too innocent to understand the law, in order to justify his double standard in dealing with his own and Tess's confession.

"Fate" in the Classical Context

When both religion and secular society "sport" with Tess in her life in the novel, we readers seem to feel that there is no possible salvation, but merely a pessimism. This pessimism seems to prevail in most of Hardy's later novels, *Tess of the D'Urbervilles*, as well as *The Mayor of Casterbridge* (1886) and *Jude the Obscure* (1895). As discussed above, if anyone in any episode of the novel, either religiously or secularly, had selected to break the stereotype Tess could have been saved.[13] As a reader like myself from such a complex cultural system as China where Confucius seldom talks about fate, Zhuangzi shows an attitude to respond to everything that comes to him with much more equanimity, I cannot but help think that it is "fate," the inescapable iron force, that is "sporting" ultimately with Tess, although

---

12. Thomas Hardy, *Tess (Library Edition)*, 120–21.

13. Here it must be made clear that if any of the events in the narration of the novel relating to Tess's destiny could be changed even for one moment, Tess could be saved. The novel is full of accidents, incidents, or coincidences on which again and again Tess's tragic fate depends, and "one or two of these may seem possible—life after all is full of mischance—but heaped on top of each other they produce a final effect of gross improbability." See "Accident and Coincidence in 'Tess of the D'Urbervilles,'" in Drabble, *Genius*, 74.

Hardy reminds us time and again that determinism is something he cannot accept.

At the very end of the first phase of the novel, Hardy writes:

> As Tess's own people down in those retreats are never tired of saying among each other in their fatalistic way: "It was to be." There lay the pity of it.[14]

As a common farm girl who has been given a poor education, Tess believes in the "fatalistic way" like other poor people in the Vale of Blackmoor, and probably that is the very reason that she would not escape when finally she is cornered in Stonehenge, where her tragic life is brought to an end. However, this kind of acceptance of the "fatalistic way" is inextricably mixed with religious elements and social rules, because, the novelist soon admits that there is "an immeasurable social chasm" that divides Tess's life before Trantridge and after it. One could also argue that in *Tess of the D'Urbervilles* it is the countryside people who are mostly believers in fatalism, a belief which is certainly related to their poverty and to the fact that a peasant or a farmer has little chance to fight against such disasters as flood, plague or disease.[15] After Tess and her three friends from the dairy farm are carried by Angel, one by one, through the pool on their way to church, her friends are unhappy because they think it is obvious now that Angel is fond of Tess above the rest:

> The gaiety with which they had set out had somehow vanished; and yet there was no enmity or malice between them. They were generous young souls; they had been reared in the lonely country nooks where fatalism is a strong sentiment, and they did not blame her.[16]

Another pertinent example to show that Hardy seems to suggest that peasants or those who work on the land are more prone to believe in

---

14. Hardy, *Tess (Library Edition)*, 91.

15. Scholars have pointed out that in Hardy's early novels, traditional material such as local superstitions, seasonal rites, or festivals are used simply as "local colour to establish a setting and perhaps the frame of mind of some of his characters" while in *Tess of the D'Urbervilles* "folk materials are selected and peculiarly suited to the story of a woman victimized by the dual standards of nineteenth-century morality." See Smith, *Novels of Thomas Hardy*, 107. Here the words "dual standards" are especially important because they are the very standards of Angel's behavior on his wedding day and also of religion and society in their way of treating such a person as Tess.

16. Hardy, *Tess (Library Edition)*, 186.

fatalism is when Angel and Tess have decided upon their marriage date. The narrator comments that "her naturally bright intelligence had begun to admit the fatalistic convictions common to field-folk and those who associate more extensively with natural phenomena than with their fellow-creatures."[17] Faced with this "field-folk" fatalism, which is "inevitably" the cause of pessimism in Hardy's later novels, Tess's situation could not but end in one way—heading for the hangman's rope, an extremely bleak end where one could do nothing as Elizabeth-Jane at the end of *The Mayor of Casterbridge* says:

> But there's no altering—so it must be.[18]

Hardy may not have believed absolutely in fatalism. However, as a reader from Chinese culture, I would certainly hold to the idea that Tess is the victim of fate, otherwise she could have been saved either religiously or secularly; as discussed above any one episode in the narration might have prevented her from walking to her tragic end. Then, is this fate that the "President of the Immortals" brings about? A close reading of the history of the idea of fate and the association of Aeschylus's play with Greek culture would reveal that the concept of fate in Hardy comes from the heart of the Greco-Roman tradition.[19]

According to the *Barnhart Dictionary of Etymology*, the English word "fate" is probably formed either by the borrowing of the Old French *fat* (meaning "fate or destiny"), or it is directly formed from the Latin word *fātum* (meaning "thing spoken by the gods"). The English word appeared about 1385 in Geoffrey Chaucer's *Troilus and Criseyde* and its derivative "fatal," interestingly, appeared about 1380 in Chaucer's translation of Boethius's *De Consolatione Philosophiae* (*The Consolation of Philosophy*), while the word "fatalism" (meaning "belief that fate controls everything that happens") appeared in 1678 and its meaning of "acceptance of everything that happens" is first recorded in 1734.[20] It is not difficult to infer that the word "fatalism" is taken from the goddesses of Roman mythology, the Fates, while it is also commonly agreed that Roman mythology is drawn,

---

17. Hardy, *Tess (Library Edition)*, 259.
18. Hardy, *Mayor of Casterbridge*, 333.
19. An interesting linkage between the discussion of Tess and the ancient Greek goddess Gaia: the material-ideological forces which produced Tess as their scapegoat retain their power; their representatives sentence Tess to death and hang her at Wintoncester gaol, so they are unquestionably guilty of Gaia's killing. See Fisher, *Hidden Hardy*, 173.
20. Barnhart, *Barnhart Dictionary*, 371.

directly or indirectly, from ancient Greek mythology. In Greek mythology the goddesses of Fate are called *Moirai*, who are generally recognized as the three daughters of the goddess Night, in age order being Klotho ("the Spinner"), Lachesis ("the Apportioner") and Atropos ("the Inevitable," the smallest in stature but also the "most terrible to be feared" in Homer's words).[21] They wear white robes and the linen thread is their representative symbol, these are easily linked with the moon and are closely connected to their name origin *Mœræ* meaning "a phase." Thus these sisters, as the Fates, are a reflection of three phases of the moon: "the new moon, the Maiden-goddess of the spring, the first period of the year; the full moon, the Nymph-goddess of the summer, the second period; and the old moon, the Crone-goddess of autumn, the last period."[22] Tradition has it that the thread (or the yarn) they spin is the "destiny of each individual in turn, and when it is broken, a life ends."[23] Another tradition suggests that the power of controlling life is even beyond the influence of Zeus, though in certain cases he can take his golden scales, usually at noon, and measure two conflicting parties to see which of them is destined to come to its end that day.[24] Yet another tradition would readily agree that Zeus, the chief deity of all gods and goddesses in classical Greek mythology, has control by weighing the lives of men and informing the Fates of his decision, thus being able to "change his mind and intervene to save whom he pleases when the thread of life, spun on Klotho's spindle, and measured by the rod of Lachesis, is about to be snipped by Atropos's shears."[25]

With the above explanation, we can come back to the question: are these Fates in fact the "President of Immortals"? In Aeschylus's *Prometheus* the words Prometheus uses when reflecting on his behavior after he is chained to a rock by the order of Zeus are surely referring to Zeus.[26] No matter whether it is the Fates who hold dominating control over a human

21. Kerenyi, *Gods of the Greeks*, 32.

22. Graves, *Greek Myths*, 48–49.

23. Rose, *Handbook of Greek Mythology*, 24.

24. Kerenyi, *Gods of the Greeks*, 32. It is worthy of note that in some versions there are only two Fates such as at Delphi, where there is only the Fate of Birth and that of Death, while at Athens, Aphrodite Urania is called the eldest of the three sisters. See Graves, *Greek Myths*, 48.

25. Graves, *Greek Myths*, 48

26. Aeschylus, *Complete Plays*, 28. In Murray's translation, the name for Zeus is "That Lord of Bliss": "The Lord of Bliss shall need me yet . . . / I swear it—in my chains and woe / To warn him of the doom I know / Shall break his sceptre and o'erset / His glories."

being's life or whether it is Zeus that is in control, Tess, at the very end of the novel, when religious elements and social standards seem to lose all their saving power, is losing her life after being "sported" with by the "President of Immortals," fate itself.[27]

As Hardy's idea of fate is closely linked to ancient Greek culture, there are some essential similarities and also fundamental differences between *Tess of the D'Urbervilles* and ancient Greek tragedies such as *Oedipus the King*. One similarity is that all the protagonists are coming to their tragic end, no matter how different their situations are, thus giving such genre of writing the name "tragedy." After discovering the truth of his accidentally killing his father and marrying his mother, Oedipus plucks out his own eyes and wanders around the world. After being deserted by Jason, whom Medea has helped to steal the golden fleece and restore his reign, Medea is thrown into such an unbearable agony that she kills her two sons by Jason with her own two hands, a stunning episode in world literature. Only by sacrificing his own daughter Iphigenia to the raging and revengeful Artemis can Agamemnon appease the wrath of the goddess. Despite this act, all ends with another family tragedy as the marshal of the Greek alliance is himself murdered by his own wife Clytemnestra and her lover Aegisthus.

All of these great ancient Greek tales are family tragedies as is the story of Tess, who is pushed by her parents to enter into the dangerous world of Alec d'Urberville ("out of the frying-pan into the fire"[28]). This is the Tess who cannot be forgiven by her husband while she already forgives him for his youthful indiscretions; the Tess who is forced to be mistress of Alec to

---

27. As mentioned at the beginning of this chapter, Hardy admits that these four words were a literal translation of two words in Aeschylus's play *Prometheus*. Because of this translation and its placement at the end of the novel, it "started a rumour of Hardy's theological beliefs, which lived, and spread, and grew, so that it was never completely extinguished" (Hardy, *Life of Thomas Hardy*, 243). As for Hardy's religious beliefs, David Jasper made the precisely wonderful conclusion: "Thomas Hardy is that most religious of beings, a man caught between belief and unbelief, something between an agnostic and an atheist, who attended the services of the Church of England to the end of his life ... and a man who could be gripped by a profound pessimism" (Jasper, *Heaven in Ordinary*, 17).

28. Hardy, *Tess (Library Edition)*, 85. These are the words said by dark Car's mother when Tess unknowingly offended the crowd and was "rescued" by Alec on their way back from the fair to the chicken farm of the d'Urbervilles. Here a perplexing thing is that in Hardy's original description dark Car's mother laughed while "stroking her moustache as she explained laconically." The sentence is odd (though deliberately so) because normally a woman would not have facial hair, and one of the Chinese translations changed the mother into "father" to make it more logical. See Hardy, *Tess* [Sun Fa-li], 65.

support the family where the father is capable of nothing but drinking and the mother is incapable of deciding anything on her part.

The second similarity is that in both *Tess of the D'Urbervilles* and most ancient Greek tragedies, the protagonists do attempt to resist their fate. When at first he knows part of the content of the oracle, Oedipus wants to escape his fate, only to find finally that he is walking into an unavoidable trap. Medea implores Creon not to banish her and her children out of the country and she also pleads with Jason about their past, only to be refused by both of them. As for Tess, her attempts to defy fate include determinedly leaving d'Urbervilles after being insulted and raped by the villain, bravely christening her child when her father closes the door upon her, fetching a clergyman, and finally killing Alec who had brought the disaster on her that caused her "impurity."

With these similarities comes one fundamental difference between these ancient Greek tragedies and *Tess of the D'Urbervilles* as far as fate or fatalism is concerned. In plays such as *Oedipus the King* invariably there is the proclaimed oracle at the beginning, or the words or arrangements of gods that are shown clearly enough, determining the hero or heroine's development of events. In *Tess*, on the other hand, the power that controls the events of Tess's life seems to be totally unknown. In other words, in *Oedipus* or in *Agamemnon*, the audience surely knows the development of events for the protagonists from the beginning, or at least they know that all the events are precisely under the control of the Olympian gods or goddesses, whereas in *Tess* the reader cannot know the later developments for Tess until they unfold chapter by chapter. With this line of thinking, I, as a Chinese reader, would extend my reflection a bit further by saying that in ancient times "fate" is "fate," and a person or even a god/goddess' mortal/immortal life events are merely controlled or organized or maneuvered by gods, a reflection of primitive times when social or religious norms or rules are still in their infancy. However, in *Tess*, an English novel written at the end of the nineteenth century, "fate," although still a mysterious and unknown force, is not only "fate" but also a phenomenon that is mixed with the often rigid demands of religious or social structures in society. In other words, living under the constraints of these religious doctrines or social rules, Tess is "fated" or destined to her tragic end while the breaking of rules, either religiously or socially, is forced upon her from the very beginning.

Then, the question arises: can these religious doctrines or social rules be altered so that Tess might be saved? In the cases of Oedipus, Medea or

Agamemnon, things cannot be changed at all and the endings for these protagonists are invariably tragic, which is a reflection of the fact that ancient people often felt simply helpless in the face of natural disasters or human miseries. While in *Tess of the D'Urbervilles*, a novel written more than two thousand years later than these great tragedies, Tess, the "pure" woman, cannot avoid her tragedy which is similar to those of her ancient predecessors but so many centuries later when civilization and society, it might be argued, have developed to such a great extent. Although at the very end of the novel it seems that in the description of Angel holding hands with 'Liza-Lu, the sister described as "a spiritualized image of Tess," Hardy is indicating a degree of hope, *Tess of the D'Urbervilles*, taken as a whole is essentially a tragedy and as for Tess, quoting Elizabeth-Jane's words in *The Mayor of Casterbridge* again, "there is no altering," it. We are as close here to pure tragedy as anywhere in English literature.

The unavoidable tragic situation in which one can do nothing at all seems to prevail in most of Hardy's later novels and this inevitable sense of fate works in a cyclic motion, which again demonstrates Hardy's seemingly absolute pessimistic outlook on life. At the end of chapter 50 of *Tess*, which is almost at the conclusion of the whole narration, there is a description, or rather the presentation of an argument about the fate of Tess's family, surely a cyclic one:

> Thus the Durbeyfields, once d'Urbervilles, saw descending upon them the destiny which, no doubt, when they were among the Olympians of the country, they had caused to descend many a time, and severely enough, upon the heads of such landless ones as they themselves were now. So do flux and reflux—the rhythm of change—alternate and persist in everything under the sky.[29]

The employment of such words as "Olympians" and "destiny" would surely evoke the association that Hardy's idea of fate, either as pessimism or fatalism, originates from ancient Greek culture, if not to be identical with it. However, what strikes me as a reader from an oriental culture, most impressively, is the connections implied in these references: the cyclic nature of history in the cause-effect chain, and the idea of change and changelessness in the events of human life. The first connotation is very near to

---

29. Hardy, *Tess (Library Edition)*, 447–48. This quote has also been used to analyze one of Hardy's experiences in London when he was exposed to the ideas of Charles Darwin and those of defenders of the Christian faith. See Webster, *On a Darkling Plain*, 27–48.

the Buddhist idea of Samsara (轮回 in Chinese), while the second one is almost the equivalent of the Taoist philosophy of "having" and "not having," of "doing" and "not doing."

"Fate" Compared in Chinese Culture

In Chinese, the character 命 or the phrase 命运 is often considered to be the equivalent of the English word "fate." In *A Beginner's Chinese-English Dictionary of the National Language (Gwoyeu)*, the explanation of 命 is "order, decree; destiny; life," with the phrase 命该如此 as "fate willed it so" and 命运 as "destiny."[30] In *A Comprehensive English-Chinese Dictionary*, "fate" is translated as "运命 (the archaic use of 命运), 天命 (literally "destiny by heaven"), (人之) 宿命 (human destiny), 命数 (the destined way), [and] 因果 (cause and effect)."[31] What is interesting here is that the above translation has at least three layers of meaning: 运命 (destiny) is the most basic meaning; 天命, 宿命 and 命数 show the meaning of "destiny or fate coming from heaven"; 因果 clearly shows the influence of Buddhism.

With the above explanation, it can be argued that in the Chinese concept of "fate" there is a basic equivalence of meaning between "fate" and 命. However, in the second layer of meaning, this equivalence becomes at best questionable, "fate" being the destiny maneuvered by the gods while 命 is destiny from heaven. The difference lies in the fact that in Chinese culture, "heaven" is a rather complicated idea. It can mean just the sky in the physical sense, or it can be an abstract figure that controls everything (for example, the Chinese would say all is destined by heaven and sometimes the image of heaven is taken as a male as in the phrase 天公, meaning literally "heaven lord or heaven sir"). But the Chinese idea of heaven is very different from the home of the Greek gods such as Zeus, or of Jehovah in the Hebrew Bible. Because of this ambiguity in concept and image, the Chinese sense of heaven is extremely difficult to pin down and therefore the sense of the destiny it imposes upon humankind is also very hard to ascertain.

The most peculiar aspect of the Chinese understanding of fate is in its third layer of meaning, which is directly linked to ideas of transmigration in Buddhism, a religion which originated in India and was accepted and

---

30. Simon, *Beginner's Dictionary*, 503. This dictionary is dedicated to Jaw Yuanren (Y. R. CHAO, 赵元任), one of the most important scholars of Chinese and Chinese dialects in the twentieth century.

31. Huang, *Comprehensive English–Chinese Dictionary*, 434.

transformed by Chinese culture after the first century. It remains a very influential force in modern China. A frustrated or depressed Chinese person might say to his or her friend who is successful and prosperous the words 你命真好 (what a good life/destiny you have), or this same person might loathe his own bad fortune and mutter the words 来世好命 (a good life/destiny in the next life). Sentences like these indicate the influence of Buddhist concepts of this life and the next life. For example, if you do a good deed in this life you will be rewarded in next life. Thus a good result in the next life is caused by this life's good deeds, fulfilling a cyclic pattern between this world and the next. This application of transmigrating meaning in the word 命, as explained above, takes place no earlier than the first century CE. However, much earlier than that time, two influential branches of religious thinking—Confucianism and Taoism—already existed in Chinese culture.

In the basic text of Confucianism, *The Analects*, Confucius talks about fate very tentatively. In Chapter IV, Book II, the Master gives his "own account of gradual progress and attainments":

> At fifteen, I had my mind bent on learning. At thirty, I stood firm. At forty, I had not doubts. At fifty, I knew the decrees of Heaven. At sixty, my ear was an obedient organ for the reception of truth. At seventy, I could follow what my heart desired, without transgressing what was right.[32]

It deserves attention here that the famous sinologist and translator of this passage James Legge rendered the original 天命 as "decrees of Heaven." In Chinese writing a capital letter has no significance, whereas in modern English writing the difference between a capitalized word and a non-capitalized word is quite obvious. As the first professor of Chinese Language and Literature in Oxford University and more importantly, as a missionary from the London Missionary Society, Legge was extremely sensitive to the cultural differences between Chinese concepts and western ideas. Here, obviously, Legge takes heaven as a special form of being which is capable of giving decrees to man, but he is also aware of the tantalizing danger of rendering it as a being that is close to Jehovah in the Bible or to Zeus in Greek mythology. Let us look at another translation of this part of *The Analects*, one also rendered by a missionary (a Methodist), William Edward Soothill, who spent a long time in China, taking the position of the Principal of

---

32. Confucius, *Confucian Analects* [Legge], 10–11.

the Shansi Imperial University and becoming the professor of Chinese in Oxford University almost fifty years later than James Legge:

> The Master said: "At fifteen I set my mind upon wisdom. At thirty I stood firm. At forty I was free from doubts. At fifty I understood the laws of Heaven. At sixty my ear was docile. At seventy I could follow the desires of my heart without transgressing the right."[33]

Compared with Legge, Soothill's translation has fewer words but it can still be seen that Soothill is under the influence of Legge's translation. As for the words 天命, Soothill's rendering is not very different from that of Legge, only changing the term "decrees" into "laws," and these can be regarded as almost synonymous in this context. In his translation, Soothill also capitalized the word "heaven," making the complicated and ambiguous Chinese 天 into a more specific and more concrete term. It seems that a tantalizing conclusion can be drawn here that Legge and Soothill, both being missionaries, tend to make the image of heaven in ancient Chinese culture more perceptible and perhaps concrete on the one hand, while keeping away from making it too close to the concept of Jehovah or Zeus in western reader's mind on the other. Later translations seem to follow that direction whether the translator is educated in a Chinese context or in a western context. For example, the famous Chinese British scholar and translator Din Cheuk Lau (刘殿爵) rendered the sentence which includes 天命 as "at fifty I [Confucius] understood the Decree of Heaven";[34] another version of the same sentence by the Chinese American scholar and translator Chichung Huang reads "at fifty, I knew the decree of Heaven," which is almost the same as Legge's translation, with an annotation "The Master knew even then that the sage kings' Way of humane government was not to prevail."[35]

A very different version of the passage quoted above by Legge and by Soothill is made by two American scholars:

> From fifteen, my heart-and-mind was set upon learning; from thirty I took my stance; from forty I was no longer doubtful; from fifty I realized the propensities of *tian* (*tianming* 天命); from sixty my ear was attuned; from seventy I could give my heart-and-mind free rein without overstepping the boundaries.[36]

---

33. Confucius, *Analects of Confucius* [Soothill], 150–51.
34. Confucius, *Analects* [Lau], 63.
35. Confucius, *Analects of Confucius* [Huang], 52.
36. Confucius, *Analects of Confucius* [Ames and Rosemont], 76–77.

The differences in this version are not difficult to discern due to its employment of Chinese *pinyin*, a system of spelling for pronunciation of Chinese characters formally drawn up in 1950s along with the establishment of Mandarin as the standard reading and writing system. For non-Chinese readers, the *pinyin* translation is certainly not comprehensible, so the translators offer an explanatory note on the passage—"The vocabulary in this passage entails the 'path (dao 道)' metaphor: striking out in a direction, taking one's place, knowing which way to go, realizing the terrain around one, following along . . . and then journeying wherever one wants without going astray."[37] Obviously, 天命 here is rendered in such a way (paying attention to words such as "path" and "way") that it is more concrete and more close to a man-made rule rather than one coming from heaven. This is also quite obvious in Chichung Huang's rendering "way." Therefore there seem to be two approaches to translating 天命: one favors the use of "decree" or "law" (of Heaven), which is to some extent more understandable to western culture, and the other favors the use of "way," which easily rouses the suspicion of suggesting the manner as to how Confucius would like the world to be ruled.

Actually, in the *Analects*, Confucius and his disciples talk about "fate" (six times in the text of the *Analects*) much less than they talk about *dao* ("way"). In almost every book of the *Analects* there is some discussion about *dao*. In Chapter VIII, Book VI, when one of his disciples is dying, Confucius holds his hand and says "it is the appointment of Heaven" (here 命 is "life" and also "fate"). In Chapter VI, Book VIII, Master Zeng, one of Confucius's most distinguished disciples, says that if a man "can be commissioned with authority over a state of a hundred *le*," he is indeed a superior man (original words 君子, literally "a gentleman"). (命 here refers to "the commands from a sovereign.") In Chapter XVIII, Book XI, when comparing two of his excellent students Confucius says that one is nearly attaining "to perfect virtue" but is always in want, while the other "does not acquiesce in the appointments of Heaven" but his goods are increased abundantly. In Chapter VIII, Book XVI, Confucius says that there are "three things of which the superior man stands in awe," that is, "awe of the ordinances of Heaven, awe of the great man and awe of the words of sages" (天命 here is closer to a religious meaning). In the last chapter of the last book in the *Analects*, the Master says that "without recognizing the ordinances of Heaven, it is impossible to be a superior man" (here James

---

37. Confucius, *Analects of Confucius* [Ames and Rosemont], 232.

Legge seems to reinforce the impression that the meaning of 天命 should be closer to a religious term).[38]

With the above examples, the summarizing passage about Confucius and his disciples' discussion about 命 is found in the following sentence:

> The subjects of which the Master seldom spoke were—profitableness, and also the appointments of Heaven, and perfect virtue (子罕言利与命与仁).[39]

Towards profitableness, Confucius holds a disdainful attitude, so he seldom talks about it. As for perfect virtue, the Master does not need to talk about it because that is one of his fundamental characteristics and in whatever he says or acts virtue is present. And as for fate, Confucius seldom talks about it, because on the one hand what "fate" or "decree" or "appointment" comes from is almost a mysterious, unknown and ambiguous being, and on the other hand, and which is more important, Confucius's focus is on the "way" of this world, that is, a Confucian way of living, governing and so on. Thus generally Confucianism is considered as a system of thought which focuses on "going into the world/reality/entity" (入世).

Against this background, when the idea of fate in Hardy's *Tess of the D'Urbervilles* is compared with that in Confucianism, it can be seen that there are similarities; fate is something which controls our life and also something that we can do nothing to prevent. But, there is a basic difference that, for Hardy, everything seems to fail when one is facing fate, while in Confucianism, at least for Confucius and his immediate disciples, since there is nothing to be done about it one's focus should be on getting on with the way of this world and this reality.

Xunzi (荀子), another famous Confucian master who lived about 300 years after Confucius, developed Confucius's idea of 天 to a more materialistic degree by stating that one can subdue the decree of heaven (that is fate) to be used by man himself (制天命而用之).

In Chinese culture, if we say that Confucianism is a kind of "going-into-world" system of thought, the contrary of that, the system of thought being "out-of-world" (出世), is found in Taoism. In Taoism, fate is again seldom discussed and when it is the idea is that one just has to accept one's fate without putting up any fight and with the focus on the attitude of

---

38. Confucius, *Confucian Analects* [Legge], 52, 74, 107, 177, 218.
39. Confucius, *Confucian Analects* [Legge], 80.

"roaming randomly and heartily" (逍遥游). In one of the essential classic texts of Taoism *Lao-Tze* (or the *Dao De Jing*) the word 命 appears only once:

> Tao is the cause; virtue, the fosterage; and then things take shape. And there must be a power that helps the shaped things to be varying and in continuation. So all things don't fail to revere Tao, and to esteem virtue. With Tao revered and virtue esteemed, everything goes natural without a command.[40]

Here, 命 means to order or command as in the two-word phrase in Chinese 命令, which is irrelevant to our discussion of "fate."[41] Lao-Tze, if we agree there is such a person, on the whole, is more concerned about the "way" of governing, including governing a state and governing oneself, the force of which, interestingly, is also given or formed by "heaven," a similar mysterious unknown element as in Confucianism. *Zhuangzi*, another pivotal scripture of Taoism, includes more discussion of 命. In some places in the text 命 is "life" and the author holds the idea that life is very precious and we have to cherish it. More often the case is that a person has to accept what happens to them (to accept one's fate), a passive acceptance which reflects the harsh conditions of survival in the Warring States period of ancient China, though more importantly it is a reflection of an attitude of "roaming randomly and heartily" because in the case of the loss of one's physical body it has been incorporated into the whole universe and in the case of suffering a tragic fate, if one tolerates the suffering, it would mean a thorough release of one's spirit thus making "roaming" possible.[42]

Therefore, it can be seen that in Taoism, "fate" is occasionally discussed and the focus for Taoism is in the philosophy of governing the self or in the attitude of achieving a certain degree of spirituality. In Taoism, "fate" can originate from heaven and one has no controlling power over it, and this is quite similar to Hardy's view in *Tess of D'Urbervilles*. However, for Hardy, one can do nothing about the inevitable "tragical condition of

---

40. Lao-Tze, *Lao-Tze in English* [Chang] (张发榕), 52.

41. Arthur Waley, the renowned Sinologist, translated the same passage as "Tao gave them birth; / The 'power' of Tao reared them, / Shaped them according to their kinds/ Perfected them, giving to each its strength. / Therefore of the ten thousand things there is not one that does not worship Tao and do homage to its 'power.' No mandate ever went forth that accorded to Tao the right to be worshipped, nor to its 'power' the right to receive homage. / It was always and of itself so" (Waley, *Way and Power*, 205). The last sentence in Waley's translation deserves our attention for it is a free translation of the Chinese 命, but it still carries the philosophical tone of the original.

42. See the detailed explanation of Zhuangzi's attitude in chapter 1 above.

life," an absolute pessimism,[43] while in Taoism, the attitude toward fate is more about a philosophy of governing or about an attitude of realizing a spiritual thoroughness.

One particular point has to be made clear here. Lao-Tze does emphasize the idea of "doing nothing" (无 为) in such phrases as "He does not contend/ And for that very reason no one under heaven can contend with him," "Tao never does; yet through it all things are done."[44] It would appear that these sentences indicate that we should do nothing about the situation we are in, usually a harsh or a tragic one. However, when we read such injunctions as "do not contend," we should be very careful not to omit the phrase which follows: "for that very reason no one under heaven can contend with him." For Lao-Tze, it is a common rhetorical device used when he observes that in the universe there seem to be many pairs of binary or complimentary phenomena such as sky and earth, man and woman, summer and winter, day and night, and this is probably one of the sources of yin and yang (阴 阳) in Taoism. More importantly, the emphasis on "doing nothing" is that by doing nothing one achieves the uttermost goal of having everything; by not contending, power rests with that person and no-one can challenge it. Therefore, the idea of "doing nothing" always accompanies the idea of "having everything," a dialectic feature characteristic of Lao-Tze, and reflects such an attitude as close to "less is more." If we investigate this idea of Taoism from social, cultural and historic perspectives, a similar conclusion can be made as when we investigate the ideas of Zhuangzi. That is, there is a reflection of the situation in the Spring and Autumn and Warring States period when people were often in danger of losing their lives and properties and ideas were often in conflict with one another.

However, in *Tess of the D'Urbervilles*, the situation is hopeless for Tess, arousing the reader's sense that one can "do nothing" about it. This is a reflection of Hardy's harsh criticism of religion (Christianity in particular) and society (Victorian morality and standards). Christians refuse to help

---

43. As Hardy himself admits, "the best tragedy—highest tragedy in short, is that of the worthy encompassed by the inevitable"(see Florence Emily Hardy, *Later Years*, 14). One scholar points out that "the conception of tragedy in *Tess of the D'Urbervilles* rests on an assumption of inevitability, in several discrete yet interrelated forms of determinism, from heredity, Nature or super nature." Besides that there is also a kind of psychological determinism in the novel, "a psychological condition, part of the ache of modernism, to be a principle determinant in the fate of romance and marriage in the culture." See Kramer, "Psychological Determinism," 135, 152.

44. Waley, *Way and Power*, 171, 188.

her. So does society with its social rules or laws. Nothing can be done and Tess is fated to her tragic ending. Therefore, from this perspective, *Tess of the D'Urbervilles* is a tragedy.[45] But is there really no hope at all? Besides the moral and religious pressure which is this very "hopelessness," or "darkest fatalism,"[46] also part of the reason that Hardy would not continue in fictional writing? Still, as a Chinese reader who would readily fall into the cliché that most Chinese literary works have happy endings, I would also readily accept that the scene of Angel holding hands with 'Liza-Lu at the very end of *Tess of D'Urbervilles* is a symbol or a hint of hope. As one scholar ponders on Hardy's poetry:

> But there is always for him a light in the darkest place, though the cost of finding it may be extreme.[47]

---

45. George Steiner holds the idea that perhaps even in Hardy's darkest fiction there is only one absolute tragedy, *The Mayor of Casterbridge*, just as Shakespeare wrote only one utterly tragic play, *Timon of Athens*. See Steiner, "Note on Absolute Tragedy," 148, quoted in Jasper, *Heaven in Ordinary*, 19.
46. Jasper, *Heaven in Ordinary*, 19.
47. Jasper, *Heaven in Ordinary*, 19.

4

Thomas Hardy and the Conflict of Cultures
A Response

David Jasper

Living within cultures involves realizing profundities of being that find echoes in depths that may be literary, sometimes forgotten but still present, and that catch us in moments that are deeply known yet barely consciously so, picked up in religious, philosophical, poetic moments that are sometimes recoverable to the intellect, often quite beyond such recovery, yet real all the same.

When *Tess of the D'Urbervilles* was published in 1891 it evoked both praise and contempt in just about equal measure. Thomas Hardy's fellow novelists Robert Louis Stevenson and Henry James exchanged private letters expressing their extreme dislike of the book. For Stevenson, *Tess* was "one of the worst, weakest, least sane, most *voulu* books I have yet read." James wrote dismissively that "the pretense of 'sexuality' is only equaled by the absence of it, and the abomination of the language by the author's reputation for style."[1] Other contemporary reviewers, however, were enthusiastic in their praise for the novel, one describing Tess as a book that "permanently enlarged the boundaries of one's intellectual and emotional

---

1. Tomalin, *Thomas Hardy*, 231.

experience."[2] It might be said that great works of art always divide opinion, though of one thing we are certain: *Tess* was an immediate best-seller and it made Hardy a rich and famous man. It cuts across many of the most sacred social, moral and religious boundaries in late Victorian society.

Hardy was one of what Basil Willey once dubbed the "honest doubters" of Victorian England.[3] He was a deeply religious man who attended church to the end of his life and yet who found the constraints of the Victorian church, and even Christianity itself, finally unworkable and unacceptable. He was profoundly pessimistic—a fatalist—who wrote books that were perhaps the only true tragedies in English literature since the plays of Shakespeare. *Tess* throws down the gauntlet to the Victorian class system, while denouncing the claims and pretences of the *nouveau riche* in the character of Alec d'Urberville. Hardy addresses the place of women in society, and especially the utter defenselessness of working-class girls like Tess. The Church of England suffers under his pen. And then there is the matter of "fate"—a preoccupation with Hardy in his poetry and his final great epic drama *The Dynasts* (1908) which Laurence Binyon described as exploring "the implanted crookedness of things."

In Florence Hardy's *Life of Thomas Hardy* (probably largely written in note form by Hardy himself), there is a lengthy comment on the celebrated sentence in the last paragraph of the novel: "The President of the Immortals, in Aeschylean phrase, had ended his sport with Tess."[4] It initiated, Florence Hardy suggests, a rumor regarding Hardy's "theological beliefs" which never quite died away, a suggestion concerning Hardy's "belief" in some willfully malicious deity who turns all human life to an evil end. In fact, she states, he was using a literal translation of Aeschylus's *Prometheus Bound* (a text to which the Victorians after Byron and Shelley were peculiarly addicted), Μακαρων πρυτανις, understanding it in the "classical sense."[5] This makes perfectly good sense given the rootedness of the late nineteenth century in classical studies, not least Aristotle's *Poetics*, a trend which continued in English education and culture well into the twentieth century.[6] But the important difference between *Tess* and Greek tragedy

2. Tomalin, *Thomas Hardy*, 230.

3. See Willey, *More Nineteenth-Century Studies*.

4. Hardy, *Tess*, 508. The quotation in Florence Emily Hardy, *Later Years*, 3, omits the phrase "in Aeschylean phrase."

5. Florence Emily Hardy, *Later Years*, 2–3.

6. See, Henn, *Harvest of Tragedy*. Henn's writing on tragedy connects closely with his work on W. B. Yeats. See below, 62, 84.

lies in the sense of plot, the Greek tragedian being rooted in and shaped by an already defined myth. Here nothing happens by chance.

Hardy, however, whose plots creak along full of daily mishap, mischance and ironic twists (like the misplaced note under the door in *Tess*), is also drawing on a pre-Elizabethan tradition of medieval tragedy—Tess, like Lear, is bound upon a wheel of fire, a plaything of fortune who is subject to the vicissitudes and accidents to which we are all prone, but she in particular according to her particular circumstances, her beauty, indeed her *goodness* which render her all the more vulnerable. The gods who sport with poor humanity must surely be an echo of Gloucester's fate in *King Lear*: "As flies to wanton boys are we to the gods; they kill us for their sport."[7] The image is significant. Such "gods" are nothing, to be reduced to mere, thoughtless children, lacking in any moral sense, who willfully pull the wings off flies. The world of *Tess of the D'Urbervilles* (far more than that of *The Mayor of Casterbridge* or even *Jude the Obscure*) sounds an echo of what G. Wilson Knight long ago called the "Lear universe," with its "down-pressing, enveloping presence" which, in *Lear* and *Tess*,

> has no personal symbol, it is not evil, nor good; neither beautiful, nor ugly. It is purely a brooding presence, vague, inscrutable, enigmatic; a misty blurring opacity stilly overhanging, interpenetrating plot and action. This mysterious accompaniment to the *Lear* story makes of its persons vague symbols of universal forces. But those persons, in relation to their setting, are not vague.[8]

This almost works for *Tess of the D'Urbervilles*, but not quite, perhaps. At times Hardy and Shakespeare share a tragic vision of life, and arguably *Timon of Athens* and *The Mayor of Casterbridge* are, indeed, the only two absolute tragedies in the English language.[9] But Hardy's sense of fate and his pessimism are not of the English Renaissance, being more immediately grounded in that late Victorian loss of faith which is greater and more complex than simply a parting of the ways from Christian assurance and belief. Tess, after all, is a "pure woman" in a world that is both changing and yet still addicted to old assumptions about marriage, religion, class, gender and a thousand other things that we, as latter-day Victorians,[10] still trail around

---

7. Shakespeare, *King Lear* 4.1.36–37.

8. Knight, *Wheel of Fire*, 178.

9. This was a claim once made by George Steiner in Steiner, "Note on Absolute Tragedy."

10. See Foucault, *History of Sexuality*.

with us—but how much more does Hardy. The ancient and lost heraldic world of the d'Urberville family, with its Norman origins and its country seats in Kingsbere, Sherton, Millpond, Lullstead and Wellbridge is part of an attachment to romantic history (an addiction the English have never quite shaken off, as is all too clear in our current political circumstances), while Alec d'Urberville emerges from nowhere in a new world that is often crass, brittle and superficial.

The tragedy of Tess takes place in a society that is at once moving into modernity but with an unwillingness that finds it hard to let go of the old structures that once seemed to hold it all together. In other words, this is a world in dislocation, caught between religious belief and unbelief and therefore all the more prone to prejudice and superstition. Nothing could be further (inasmuch as I, as a Western observer, can understand the concept at all) from the Taoist concept of *wu wei*—doing nothing or not doing. Tess is very far from the final world of Fugui in Yu Hua's post Cultural Revolution novel *To Live* (1993).[11] Fugui, in his acceptance of all that life can throw at him, is a man who is determinedly alive, while Tess's death hangs like a shadow over all her life. She is pursued relentlessly by her fate, while the "doing nothing" of *wu wei* "far from being an attitude of passive acceptance or resignation . . . is instead an active engagement with things as they are."[12] That is to live, in Taoist culture, finally, within the harmony of all things. But Tess knows only dislocation—and perhaps, at second hand, some distant hope in the future of Angel Clare and 'Liza-Lu, but a hope without much consolation, and none for Tess herself. For the echoes of the end of Milton's *Paradise Lost* in the final sentence of the novel remind us that we live in a fallen world:

> As soon as they had strength they arose, joined hands again, and went on.[13]

Tess of the D'Urbervilles, like all great tragedies, strikes a universal chord in all readers, and yet it remains quintessentially of its time and place—England in the Victorian era. It has become part of English consciousness so that Claire Tomalin has written that "Tess's name is embedded in the consciousness even of people who have never read the book."[14]

---

11. See below, 128–29.
12. Chuang Tzu, *Inner Chapters*, xvi.
13. Hardy, *Tess*, 508.
14. Tomalin, *Thomas Hardy*, 227.

In its day it made Hardy famous—he was elected to membership of the Athenaeum Club in London—and became a member of the highest society in the capital city. That same society argued about Tess at fashionable dinner parties. The Duchess of Abercorn divided her guests between those who thought Tess to be "a little harlot" who deserved to be hung, and those who call her a "poor wronged innocent" and pitied her.[15] And further, its fame made Hardy an international celebrity across Europe, America and Asia. It was quickly translated into Russian. And so what of Hardy and fate? I am inclined to think that in the end he was simply a pessimist, a man for whom, despite his success, the world was out of joint, its accidents beyond the reach of moral explanation or religious justification. But the elements of Greek tragedy are ineradicable. Florence Hardy noted of one of Hardy's distinguished visitors:

> Dr. Walter Lock, Warden of Keble Oxford called. "*Tess*," he said, "is the Agamemnon without the remainder of the Oresteian trilogy." This is inexact, but suggestive as to how people think.[16]

Would *Tess* have ever been possible in the ancient culture of China? I think not, in the end.

---

15. Florence Emily Hardy, *Later Years*, 6.
16. Florence Emily Hardy, *Later Years*, 8.

5

Religious Perspectives in Yeats's Poetry[1]

Ou Guang-an

IN 1923, THE IRISH poet William Butler Yeats (1865–1939) was awarded the Nobel Prize in Literature and the commending address by the award committee was "for his always inspired poetry, which in a highly artistic form gives expression to the spirit of a whole nation."[2] Some years later, another Nobel Prize winner in Literature, T. S. Eliot praised Yeats as "the greatest poet of our time—certainly the greatest in this language,"[3] while Ezra Pound, one of Yeats's close friends in the early twentieth century, claims that Yeats was the most important poet in that era, demanding our full attention. After centuries of Irish suffering under English colonial rule, Yeats's winning of this prestigious and influential international award was of particular importance both for himself and for Ireland.[4] However, the religious elements of this great poet who has been accredited as creating a new national "Irish-English" literature,[5] have often been ignored or taken for granted by academic studies in criticism. The fact remains, however,

1. Substantial content from this chapter was previously published in *Thought & Culture* 20 (2017) 110–30.

2. Yeats, "Preface," 1.

3. The words are from a speech addressed by T. S. Eliot in the Abbey Theatre in 1940, a year after Yeats's death. See Hall and Steinmann, *Permanence of Yeats*, 331.

4. The award of the Nobel prize was just one year after Eire became an independent country. The timing may not be insignificant.

5. Later, "Irish-English Literature" is also called "Anglo-Irish Literature," which means the literature of Irish writers written in English in order to differentiate it from literature written in Gaelic by Irish writers.

that Yeats's writing is invariably bound with his country, Ireland, where strong religious adherence either to Catholicism or Protestantism was a prominent aspect of national life at the end of nineteenth century and the beginning of twentieth century when Yeats was writing the majority of his poetry.

Since the 1930s, study of Yeats's verse has been through a process of focusing on the formalistic aspects of the poetry to a broader cultural poetic perspective.[6] Early British critics such as Angus Wilson and W. H. Auden ponder on Yeats's poems from such perspectives as symbolist writing techniques and poetic narrative styles,[7] while later critics such as Cleanth Brooks do the analysis using their own analytic tools such as attention to "texture."[8] One of the most important academic publications on Yeats at that time is the volume entitled *The Permanence of Yeats* (1950), edited by James Hall and Martin Steinman, which includes almost all of the significant criticism on Yeats's poetry from the New Critical perspectives in the 1940s and 1950s.[9] After that, two distinguished experts on Yeats began to show their influence. R. Ellmann and A. Norman Jeffares, both emphasized the textual analysis of Yeats's works (especially poetry) as well as focusing on Yeats's life experience and biographical materials.[10] In the

---

6. This paper takes the view of Professor Wang Lixin, expert in Hebrew Biblical studies and western literature in Nankai University, as the analytic perspective. Prof. Wang points out that form poetics is a criticism focusing on textual analysis with such representative schools as Formalism and New Critics while cultural poetics is a criticism focusing on analysis of historical and cultural factors. He also emphasizes that "classic" research should be done using a combination of these two approaches, forming a kind of "organic unity view." See Wang Lixin, "Classic Quality and Methods," 28.

7. Wilson, *Axel's Castle*; Holdeman, *Cambridge Introduction to Yeats*, 118.

8. Brooks, *Well Wrought Ur*.

9. This book included essays by such prominent critics as Wilson and Blackmore from Yeats's early times, J. C. Ransom, Allen Tate, and Austin Warren, representative of New Critics, as well as T. S. Eliot, W. H. Auden, F. R. Leavis, etc.

10. Richard Ellmann made his name doing research on Yeats, but later he transferred his attention to James Joyce and Oscar Wilde. He acquired some valuable material given by Mrs Yeats, which had never been published, and wrote two famous books on Yeats. See Ellmann, *Yeats: Man and the Masks*; *Identity of Yeats*. A. Norman Jeffares began the tradition of annotating every poem by Yeats by publishing *Commentary on the Collected Poems of W. B. Yeats* in 1968, and very soon he published the newly revised version, *New Commentary*. Jeffares's biographical study of Yeats combined with criticism on Yeats's poetry includes *W. B. Yeats: Man and Poet*; *W. B. Yeats: New Biography*. Jeffares was also a great compiler of Yeats's poems, either complete or in selection anthology, and these compilation works have become authoritative sources on Yeats study. There are also some other important research works by contemporaries of Ellmann and Jeffares, for example, Henn, *Lonely Tower*; Unterecher, *Reader's Guide*.

1970s Harold Bloom emerged as one of the representatives in Yeats study with the publication of *Yeats* (1970), which is a typical and excellent example of Bloom's critical idea of the "anxiety of influence," demonstrating in great detail the influence on Yeats of such eminent poets as Blake and Shelley.¹¹ After that, study on Yeats transfers its direction to the background and poetic resources that help to explain and illustrate his poems. That is, the focus is diverted from the form of the poetry to something more like cultural poetics. Amy Geraldine Stock puts her interest in a discussion of the relation between Yeats's poetry and his poetics. Marjorie Howes focuses her research on ideas of nation, gender and class in Yeats, and Vereen M. Bell tries to make clear the formalist logic in Yeats's works.¹² In the 1980s a book by Elizabeth Cullingford focused on the discussion of Yeats and Fascism, attracting some attention in the academic world,¹³ but most studies would agree that it is quite unfair to relate Yeats's writing on power and authority to fascism. Since the 1950s, a series of biographical works on Yeats have been published, but none can compare with the two large volumes by R. F. Forster.¹⁴ In the most recent two decades, there seems to have been a tendency to return to the formalist poetic approach in research on Yeats alongside the continuance of a cultural poetics perspective.¹⁵

In the field of international scholarship, research on Yeats and his works begins quite late in China and there are not many prominent achievements so far, the majority of work focusing on Yeats's artistic technique in poetry writing.¹⁶ Reflecting comprehensively on the above research, it might be said that research on specific texts and on historic and cultural factors on the formation of Yeats's works has achieved a great deal, but one perspective

11. Bloom, *Yeats*.

12. See Stock, *W. B. Yeats*; Howes, *Yeats's Nation*; Bell, *Yeats Logic of Formalism*.

13. See Cullingford, *Yeats, Ireland, and Fascism*. There are two more recent books which discuss Yeats's attitude toward violence and fascism: Wood, *Yeats and Violence*; McCormack, *Blood Kindred*. See also Larrissy, "Yeats in Light of Recent Criticism," 12.

14. Besides the books by Ellmann and Jeffares, there are also such prominent biographical works as Archibald, *Yeats*; Brown, *Life of W. B. Yeats*. R. F. Foster's two volumes were published in 1997 and 2003 respectively. See Foster, *Yeats*.

15. See Rosenthal, *Running to Paradise*; Vendler, *Our Secret Discipline*.

16. The most important and authoritative research results have been obtained by Fu Hao, a renowned scholar who works in the Department of Foreign Languages and Literature, Chinese Academy of Social Science. He not only translated all lyric poems by Yeats and revised them time and again for twenty years but also wrote such important books as *Yeats*. The author of this paper has also published two books on Yeats. See Ou Guang-an, *Nation, Theme, Identity*; *Borrowing and Incorporation*.

has been ignored deliberately or otherwise, and that is, the dimension of religion in the analysis of the poetry.[17] Fu Hao's paper "Christian Elements in Yeats's Works" is one of the most insightful observations on the subject, putting emphasis on Christian settings, allusion, and quotation in Yeats's works and drawing the conclusion that Yeats puts Christianity and other religions at the same level, employing all of them as his writing material. Dwight Hilliard Purdy's book *Biblical Echo and Allusion in the Poetry of William Butler Yeats* (1994) lists almost all the biblical allusions and stories in Yeats's poems, making it the most complete and comprehensive book listing biblical elements in Yeats's works so far. However, the author does not discuss in depth and in detail the specific religious perspective Yeats takes in his writing and the reasons for that.[18] There are also some papers or chapters sparsely scattered in various journals and books on Yeats's religious perspective in writing, which are either fragmentary in form or lack real focus. When taking a closer look at the question of religion, I would argue that perhaps it is because Yeats's poetic technique is too overwhelmingly prominent so that his other identities are concealed or possibly it is because Yeats's idea on religion is too straightforward when compared with such writers as T. S. Eliot, thus it can be taken for granted. However, the fact remains that in Yeats's works religious elements such as biblical setting, allusion, stories are so often apparent[19] that one might argue that they constitute some kind of deep psychological reflection in Yeats's literary output.

Yeats's paternal ancestors were Protestants from England who moved to Ireland, and Yeats's family was attached to the Protestant state Church of Ireland for many years. Yeats's maternal family were also Protestant, most of them being merchants and wealthier than Yeats's father's family. Influenced by his father and the times in which he lived, Yeats himself was not a pious Protestant. In Yeats's Ireland, the Protestants constituted the ruling class although the majority of Irish common people were Catholics. In this special cultural context Yeats inevitably fell under the influence of both Protestantism and Catholicism writing with inevitably religious elements consciously or unconsciously in his works. With the textual analysis of representative poems of different stages of Yeats's poetry and the historical and cultural

---

17. So far as the author of this essay knows, there is still not a specialized book on the discussion of religion in Yeats's works.

18. See Purdy, *Biblical Echo and Allusion*.

19. According to Purdy, in the 374 lyric poems by Yeats (see Finneran's edition of collected poems of Yeats), 115 are related to the King James Bible and 265 Biblical allusions have been used. See Purdy, 24.

investigation of life experience and background in writing these poems, I would argue that Yeats's poetry passes through roughly three stages as far as his religious views are concerned. In his early poetry Yeats seems to enjoy mocking Catholics while agreeing with the position of the Protestant Church of Ireland. In the poetry of his middle period, for some time, he advocates the equal status of different denominations and in the later poetry he seems to return to the attitude of his early writing, reflecting his developing and changing attitude towards religion. Along with reflection on politics, reality, culture, history and so on, Yeats constructs his world of affinity to "Ascendency"—a state of "ruling" or "governing" with the Protestant aristocracy at the center.

Early Poetry

Born in 1865 in Dublin, Yeats was the eldest son of John Butler Yeats, whose ancestors were English Protestants moving to Ireland centuries before, including priests in their number. However, when John Butler Yeats was growing up and receiving his education, he did not take up the family tradition but chose to study law first and was later determined to be an artist, both professions being quite removed from the family tradition and expectation. Influenced by the events of his time, John himself even became a sort of skeptic in religious matters, an attitude which was passed on to his eldest son who began to show a similar skeptical spirit in his teenage years by reading the works of free-thinker evolutionists such as Charles Darwin and Thomas Henry Huxley. John's education of his children has its apparent effect on Yeats and his younger sisters and brother and many years later Yeats readily admitted he was very "religious," but that the "simple-minded religion" of his childhood (the Church of Ireland) was "deprived by Huxley and Tyndall" whom he detested. The new religion, "almost an infallible Church of poetic tradition," he found to be:

> a fardel of stories, and of personages, and of emotions, inseparable from their first expression, passed on from generation to generation by poets and painters with some help from philosophers and theologians.[20]

However, there is also a fact that cannot be ignored easily. The greater part of Ireland, at the time of Yeats, was a country where the Christian

---

20. Yeats, *Autobiographies*, 115–16.

religion (Catholic and Protestant) played a prevailing role. With this background and the family tradition of taking clerical positions in the Church, John gave his children a religious education not dissimilar to other people. Yeats was baptized in the Church of Ireland and the water used in the service, probably taken from the Jordan River, had been kept in the family's cabinet for many years. In childhood, Yeats also read such works as Ecclesiastes and the book of Revelation,[21] and when he was fifteen he was confirmed in the Protestant tradition.[22] Therefore, as a boy, Yeats was quite familiar with the Church of Ireland and with the Bible.

"The Lake Isle of Innisfree" is one of the representative lyrics in Yeats's early poetry. The poem is a wonderful piece of work describing the beautiful landscape in Sligo, the home of Yeats's mother where Yeats and his younger sisters and brother would often go for holidays, usually with their mother. The first line ("I will arise and go now, and go to Innisfree") is an imitation from the sentence pattern in 2 Samuel 3:21 ("I will arise and go, will gather all Israel unto my lord the king") and Luke 15:18 ("I will arise and go to my father"). The first half of the second line ("And I shall have some peace there") is an imitation of the sentence pattern in Deuteronomy 29:19 ("I shall have peace"). "For always night and day" follows Mark 5:5 ("and always, night and day") closely.[23] Although in later years Yeats held that his technique in imitating biblical sentence patterns was not good enough, the above examples are ample evidence to show the poet's familiarity with the language and rhythms of the Bible.

Another representative work in Yeats's early poetry, "The Wanderings of Oisin," shows the poet's links with the Church of Ireland clearly. It is normally considered as the poem that began the recognition of Yeats in London and Dublin. It is a narrative poem in the form of a dialogue between Oisin, a hero in ancient Irish mythology, and Saint Patrick, who is said, according to tradition, to have brought Catholicism into Ireland. The development of the poem is mainly achieved by the narration of Oisin in which he talks about how he is attracted by Niamh, a fairy maid in mythology, into a fairy kingdom where there are three Islands, namely, the Island of Dancing, the Island of Many Fears and the Island of Forgetfulness. Oisin spends one

---

21. Holdeman and Levitas, *W. B. Yeats in Context*, 227.

22. Kelly, *W. B. Yeats Chronology*, 5.

23. See Purdy, *Biblical Echo and Allusion*. All the poems quoted in this paper are from the edition edited by Richard J. Finneran. See Yeats, *Poems (New Edition)*. All biblical quotations are from the King James Version.

hundred years in each island and finally, when he remembers the glorious time of fighting side by side with Fenian warriors[24] he decides to go back to his homeland, with Niamh's repeated warning to him that he should not let his feet touch the earth. In the hustle and joy of returning, Oisin forgets the warning, lands on the ground accidentally and is turned into a three-hundred-year-old man. At the end of the poem, neglecting Saint Patrick's dissuasion, Oisin is determined to go to find his hero brothers:

> It were sad to gaze on the blessed and no man I loved of old there;
>   I throw down the chain of small stones! when life in my body has ceased,
>   I will go to Caolite, and Conan, and Bran, Sceolan, Lomair,
>   And dwell in the house of the Fenians, be they in flames or at feast.[25]

In studying the poem, researchers have put their focus on national history, collective memories and the construction of national cultural identity.[26] Actually this poem can also be seen as an excellent example of analysis on Yeats's religious views. Taking the whole poem as a united structure, it can be seen that the dialogue between Oisin and Saint Patrick is an imbalanced one between different "value bodies," in Mikhail Bakhtin's term. Over the nine hundred lines of the whole poem, Saint Patrick only speaks twenty-four lines, and, most peculiarly, sometimes after Oisin's long passionate narration of his adventures the saint only answers simply or reluctantly in one or two words such as "tell on." Within Bakhtin's theory, in a certain text, different characters represent different "thoughts" or cultural values and these different characters are not slaves to be randomly disposed of but are characters who have equal rights with the author. Similar to arguments or comments by the author, the arguments and comments by the different characters have their own weights and values, so there is not only one united consciousness or thought in the text but there are many independent voices. All these different voices from different "value bodies" make

24. Mythology and legends are the major components of ancient Irish literature, which is mainly composed of three parts: mythology of Tuatha De Danann against Fomorii; legends of Cuchulainn and other Ulster heroes; and stories of Fionn mac Cumhail and Fianna—legends of Fenian heroes. (In the nineteenth century the name of the Fenian movement in Ireland is from this system of stories). These legends and stories can be categorized as the above three systems but also can be overlapping.

25. Yeats, *Poems (New Edition)*, 386.

26. See, Ding Bingwei, "Memory Recovery and History Reconstruction," 133–34; Yang Qiujuan, "Construction of National Cultural Identity," 49–50.

up the polyphony of the text.²⁷ As for "The Wanderings of Oisin," obviously Oisin represents the national or local cultural "value body" of Ireland while Saint Patrick is the "value body" that represents Christianity (Catholic in particular, but which here also symbolizes Britain in a colonial context). It seems that the dialogue between these two characters is a failed or ineffective one in which not only is Oisin not converted by Saint Patrick but also it seems that at the end of the poem Oisin is actually defying the saint. Thus it can be seen that the attitude taken by Yeats toward Catholicism is a satirical one, and this can be seen more obviously if we take Yeats's family tradition in the service of the Church of Ireland into consideration. With his satirical attitude toward Catholicism, Yeats's inclination to the Church of Ireland becomes more apparent.

If we say the tone in "The Wanderings of Oisin" is a satirical one, the attitude toward Catholicism in some other early poems by Yeats is more critical, mainly the poems relating to Parnell and to the events caused by J. M. Synge's comic play *The Playboy of the Western World* (1907). Charles Stewart Parnell, the leader of the Irish home rule movement in the latter half of the nineteenth century, was born into a Protestant landed family and by his efforts Ireland was moving towards the stage of home rule. However, with the exposure of his scandal with Mrs. O'Shea and even though the fact remains that Mrs. O'Shea had been separated from her husband for many years, Parnell's living with Mrs. O'Shea was considered by many Irish as indecent and unforgivable. In the wake of this, Parnell lost his seat in Parliament and also his leadership in the home rule movement and he died not long after. Towards this event and towards Parnell, Yeats's attitude is very clear. He calls the Catholics who blame and criticize Parnell "a frenzied crowd" and their behavior "popular rage" and "hysterica passio" ("Parnell's Funeral"). The poet wrote with a heavy heart that if people were to show more compassion and sympathy for Parnell and move forward under Parnell's instruction, then "no civil rancor [would have] torn the land apart."²⁸ In this poem it is obvious that Yeats feels great sympathy for Parnell, who comes from the same religious tradition as Yeats, and he closely links Parnell to the future of Ireland, while showing his dissatisfaction and criticism of Catholicism in Ireland to the same degree.

Poems related to Synge's play *The Playboy of the Western World* reflect a more critical tone toward Catholicism by Yeats. This play by Synge,

---

27. Bahktin, "Problems of Dostoevsky's Poetics," 4.
28. Yeats, *Poems (New Edition)*, 279–80.

one of Yeats's closest friends, is a custom comedy performed at the Abbey Theatre. The performance caused a riot in the audience because the vivid description of life in western islands was too unorthodox for the conservative Catholic audience to accept and the direct triggering of the riot came from Synge's use of word "shift" in the play. The audience (the majority of them Catholic) thought that this word was vulgar and shameful when used in such a play and even Synge was scolded as an "old snot," a distinctly insulting word.[29] The reality was that it was the vivid characterization and description of customs that bothered the majority Catholic body. When the riot happened, Yeats was speaking in Scotland and he heard from another friend, Lady Gregory, by telegraph that when the audience heard the word "shift" there was uproar. Some nationalists added to the flame of the riot by stating that Synge's play was a result of moral corruption and Synge had humiliated Irish women in front of the whole of Europe.[30] Yeats hurried back to Dublin immediately and defended Synge in front of the audience on the stage of the Abbey by emphasizing an individual's freedom of speech (Synge, as a writer, included), suggesting to the audience that they did not understand what art was and holding that there should be a distance between art and politics. In the poem "On Those that hated 'The Playboy of the Western World,' 1907," Yeats described some of the audience as "eunuchs" who "ran through Hell" and "met on every crowded street to stare upon great Juan riding by, staring upon his sinewy thigh,"[31] "Eunuchs" are impotent, and he suggests that the audience lacked ability in artistic appreciation, while ironically and hypocritically they are "cursing" the playwright and staring at his sinewy thigh (symbolizing strong sexuality) at the same time. Moreover, Yeats criticized the nationalists who confused politics with art and literature, reflecting their own impotence and inability in artistic creation when faced with Synge's genius in writing. With such a strong critical attitude toward the Catholic majority in the audience, Yeats selected such radical words against them like "Paudeen" and "Biddy," both of which are jesting, or even insulting, names for common Irish people. In "September 1914," Yeats mocked the newly rising Catholic middle class, whose aim in life was to make money only by fumbling "in a greasy till" and "adding the halfpence to the pence until drying the marrow from the

---

29. The insulting words come from a female cleaner in the Abbey Theatre, and her sentence is "Isn't Mr. Synge a bloody old snot to write such a play." See Tuohy, *Yeats*, 130.

30. Fu, *Yeats*, 112.

31. Yeats, *Poems (New Edition)*, 111.

bone."[32] Yeats even wrote a poem simply entitled "Paudeen," denouncing the populace who were disagreeing with him as having "fumbling wits." These harsh comments about Catholics were not exceptional, but they were written side by side with other words praising friends who were Protestants in such poems as the Coole Poems and the poems related to Parnell.

To some extent, for Yeats, Coole Park, the estate owned by Lady Gregory, became symbolic of the Protestant aristocracy. In "The Seven Woods," Yeats writes about the cooing sound made by groups of pigeons which is almost like the sound of a "faint thunder" while bees are humming in the garden, all of which can make the poet forget the culture of "commonness." Those wild swans in "The Wild Swans at Coole, 1919" are "brilliant creatures" which float on the quiet water, mysterious and beautiful. The poet writes with emotion that although nineteen years have passed since his first arrival at the park, these fifty-nine wild swans have not changed, still being elegant, mysterious and full of passion. These swans are symbols of eternal art and the owner of the park, Lady Gregory, is the symbol of an elegant Protestant aristocracy. In "To a Friend whose work has come to Nothing," the poet comforts this elegant friend (Lady Gregory) by calling her "being honour bred" and telling her that she does not need to compete with "any brazen throat" and her fighting for artistic cause is "the most difficult of all things known." In Coole Park, there is also a noble rider, that is, Lady Gregory's only son Robert Gregory, who does not need to use a saddle and harness in horse racing, who can ride impetuously across a dangerous place, can make friends' eyes close with fear in hunting and whose thought is quicker than a horse's feet. Robert Gregory, the rider, the scholar and a soldier, undoubtedly has all the features of a true noble man, and he was, of course, born into a prominent Protestant family.

Lady Gregory and her son are not the only aristocrats that are praised by Yeats as ideal. Sir Hugh Lane is another, who had a broad reputation as a generous man in donating money for artistic causes. However, his generous acts were often misunderstood by Catholic followers. In "To a Wealthy Man who promised a Second Subscription to the Dublin Municipal Gallery if it were proved the People wanted the Pictures," the poet describes Sir Hugh Lane as a person who "knew better how to live" than these "Paudeens and Biddies" and what he did for the artistic cause is "what the exultant heart calls good." In "An Appointment," Sir Hugh Lane is acclaimed by the poet as having a "fierce tooth and cleanly limb." Besides Sir Hugh, as discussed

---

32. Yeats, *Poems (New Edition)*, 118.

above, Parnell, the national leader for the home rule movement, who was born into minor Protestant aristocracy, was also a great person who deserved admiration and praise in Yeats's mind. In "To a Shade" Yeats praises Parnell highly for his "passionate serving," and what Parnell left is "loftier thought, sweeter emotion." In contrast, the poet scolds stubborn Catholic followers (Parnell's enemies) as "old foul mouth" who "had set the pack (of hounds)" upon Parnell so viciously that in the end what Parnell had been working so hard to gain is being destroyed by "insults and pains."

With the above close reading of some representative poems in Yeats's early poetic writings, the conclusion can be made that Yeats held something like a satirical and critical attitude towards Catholicism and its followers while knowingly or unknowingly drawing closer to Protestantism and the Church of Ireland in particular. However, his religious attitude changed somewhat in his middle poetry.

Middle Poetry

Yeats's attitude towards religion as exhibited in his fifth book of poetry, *The Green Helmet and Other Poems* (1910), had not changed greatly from his early poetry, though there is a slight difference reflected in some of the poems. But in the poems of his sixth collection entitled *Responsibilities* (1914)[33] the poet's attitude shows a quite different aspect, that is, Catholicism and Protestantism being of equal importance as "all men are equal in front of God."

In "Paudeen," Yeats's idea of equality for religious bodies emerges, though to a very tentative degree. Here the poet criticizes those common people who do not understand art. But at the end of the poem the poet suddenly realizes that "all are [equal] in God's eye" and the fact that even though there is a noisy sound there is also "a single soul" that can have "a sweet crystalline cry." The series of poems sometimes called the Beggar Poems, including "The Three Beggars," "Beggar to Beggar Cried," and

---

33. In his lifetime, Yeats kept revising and rewriting his old poems, and this is especially obvious in his later writing. So usually there are different versions of a poem. The internationally accepted approach is to arrange his collection of poems in the following order: *Crossway* (1889), *The Rose* (1893), *The Wind Among the Reeds* (1899), *In the Seven Woods* (1904), *The Green Helmet and Other Poems* (1910), *Responsibilities* (1914), *The Wild Swans at Coole* (1919), *Michael Robartes and the Dancer* (1921), *The Tower* (1928), *The Winding Stair and Other Poems* (1933), *Parnell's Funeral and Other Poems* (1935), *New Poems* (1938), and *The Last Poems* (1938–1939).

"Running to Paradise," reflect more obviously Yeats's change in religious attitude—that all people are equal before God. In the first stanza of "The Three Beggars," there is a bird, "the old crane of Gort," who stands in the river and who is looking down upon the water for little fish, from "break of day" but only "rubbish" comes his way. Then in the middle of the poem there are the stories of a king and three beggars, serving as a metaphor to satirize the common people's futile fantasy. At the end of the poem, the old crane finally understands that no matter whether you are a king or a beggar you are all the same. Similarly in the river, although it is full of rubbish, somewhere a trout may appear. At the beginning of "Beggar to Beggar Cried," the beggar imagines that if he is lucky enough he will have a good house, marry a beautiful girl and become a rich man, but in the end he realizes that even in the best houses there may be devils, pretty girls may cause trouble and the rich man can come to harm by his property. At the very end the beggar concludes that only in the Garden of Eden or Paradise can he become respected at his ease and "hear amid the garden's nightly peace." In the third line of each stanza in the poem "Running to Paradise," the poet repeats the words "I am running to Paradise" and says that there both a king and a rich man are just like a beggar.

Besides the idea of "equality" of all men before God (and thus, by implication, the equality of Catholic and Protestant), Yeats also changed somewhat his earlier satirical attitude toward Catholicism into a more tolerant one, and he even praised some of the Catholics in Ireland in his poetry. In the Easter of 1916, a volunteer army based on the Irish Republican Brotherhood instigated an uprising in Dublin. The majority of the army was Catholic, including some of the leaders, and fifteen of the leaders were finally executed by the British army. As far as his political view is concerned, before this event Yeats was a supporter of British rule in Ireland, but with the outbreak of the uprising and the courage shown by the officers and soldiers of the volunteer army, Yeats, as with some others who previously held similar opinions, changed his mind and became supportive of the independence movement for a time. Yeats heaped praise upon these nationalist officers and soldiers and even came to the radical opinion that violent force is sometimes necessary. In the poem "Easter, 1916," the poet praises the leaders of the uprising: Pierce for his energetic activities in education and in his brilliant poetic thinking and MacDonagh for his quick wit and bold, clear thought. The most obvious change in his attitude toward Catholics is shown in the description of John MacBride ("Foxy Jack") in the poem. MacBride was a Catholic nationalist. In his twenties Yeats began to express his love for Maud Gonne, a radical nationalist though born into a Protestant family, and many times he asked for her hand in marriage, only to be refused by her. Gonne later married MacBride having converted to Catholicism in order to do so. For a long time Yeats held MacBride in contempt and also held a deep grudge against him for some of his activities. At the beginning of the poem Yeats says that he once called MacBride "a drunken, vainglorious lot" who had done some terrible things to a sweet heart (Maud Gonne). But the uprising in Dublin changed the poet's attitude toward this "drunkard," suggesting that MacBride "is changed, changed utterly" and with the uprising "a terrible beauty is born." In the last lines of the poem the poet praises the leaders of the uprising and states that as long as men in Ireland come together Ireland will enjoy eternity both "now and in time to be." In another poem which is related to the Easter Uprising of 1916, "Sixteen Dead Men," Yeats praises again these leaders of the uprising and compares them to the great leaders in the uprising of 1789. The poet states that only these leaders have the quality to proclaim "our give and take" and to "converse bone to bone." The poem "Rose Tree" develops in the form of a dialogue between the uprising leaders Pearse and Connolly. Both agree that "words are lightly spoken" while taking action is far from easy, and a breath of political words may "wither" their "Rose Tree" (symbolizing Ireland). At the end of the poem, these two leaders agree that when all the "wells are parched away" there is nothing but their "own red blood" which can make a right "Rose Tree"—that is the independence of Ireland.

From holding the idea that "all men are equal before God" to the praise of these Catholic leaders and soldiers in the 1916 Easter Uprising, Yeats's religious attitude changed from his earlier poetry, that is, from his support for the Protestant Church of Ireland while satirizing Catholics, to upholding equality in different denominations and praising the bravery of Catholics.

Late Poetry

The year 1922 witnessed both the creation of the Irish Free State (ending British rule in all but Northern Ireland) and Yeats being selected as a senator. In the very next year Yeats was awarded the Nobel Prize for Literature. In his middle years, Yeats's major business, besides writing, was the management of the Abbey Theatre. After assuming the role of a public figure,

Yeats had to take on more and more political and social responsibilities. After the coming of independence, the influence of the Church of Ireland declined and more and more Catholics were elected to parliament. Increasingly social business was dealt with by Catholic members of parliament, which was often the cause of conflict between them and Protestant members of parliament. In contrast to his religious attitude in his middle period of poetry, in his later poetry Yeats returned to a more positive recognition of Protestantism.

Yeats once had a heated discussion with Catholic members of parliament about the law of marriage. After the coming of the Free State, the Irish Parliament passed an act that banned divorce, an obvious reflection of Catholic influence in the parliament. Naturally Yeats was against the act, and this was expressed both in public speeches delivered in parliament and in articles written for newspapers. Thus, Yeats was opposed to a body representative of the majority of the Irish population, the Catholics. This attitude of Yeats is most clearly seen in two series of poems: the Crazy Jane Poems and the Ribh Poems. In "Crazy Jane and the Bishop," Jane, a sharp-tongued girl who is given to satire, indicts the crimes committed by a Catholic bishop. When she was young, the bishop was not even in the position of parish priest. Clutching "an old book" (the Bible) in his fist he said that people lived like "beast and beast." The bishop's appearance is so ugly that his skin "wrinkled like the foot of a goose." He wears a "holy black" robe but it cannot hide his back which is like a "heron's hunch." This hypocritical bishop drives Jane's lover Jack away and drives Jane herself crazy. In "Crazy Jane talks with the Bishop," the bishop becomes even worse. One day, when Crazy Jane meets the bishop on the road, the bishop insults Jane saying that her "breasts are flat and fallen." Clearly the bishop knows that Crazy Jane has nowhere to go or to live, but he tells Jane to "live in a heavenly mansion, not in some foul sty." Jane's answer constructs a remarkable contrast to the words of the bishop and makes the bishop's ugliness more stunning: "fair and foul are near of kin," and even in her lowliness and poverty her pride is in the "lofty heart."

In one of the Ribh poems, "Ribh denounces Patrick," Yeats shows his satirical attitude toward Catholics again by criticizing Saint Patrick. Ribh suggests that Patrick has been crazed by "an abstract Greek absurdity" and formed that "masculine Trinity" (man, woman, child in Yeats's words), showing Yeats's criticism of Patrick for being too stubborn in keeping to

Catholic doctrines while ignoring the real situation of life.[34] In "The Pilgrim," a traveler (the pilgrim) who has fasted for some forty days on bread and buttermilk walked upon the stones "round Lough Derg's holy island," the place where it is said that Saint Patrick fasted. Here the traveler meets an old man (clearly Saint Patrick himself), who says nothing but some unrecognizable and meaningless words—"but fol de rol de rolly O." At the end of the poem, the pilgrim not only is not moved by the saint, but also decides to give up fasting and returns to his earlier dissolute life. What a criticism of Catholicism!

Besides satire and derision against Catholics, Yeats once even called the Catholic majority "mobs" who wanted to make Ireland into a country ruled by the Church after becoming a free state. In the poem "Church and State," the poet laments that mobs put the power of the Church and that of the State under their feet and worries that if these so-called supporters of the Church and the State are just a mob which "howls at the door" what will Ireland become? In "Come Gather Round Me Parnellites," the poet denounces those politicians and bishops who have pushed the overthrow of Parnell by painstakingly disclosing Parnell's private life, and most indignantly Yeats scolded that "husband" (Mr. O'Shea) who first sold and then betrayed his wife.

Along with the critical and satirizing attitude toward Catholics in Yeats's later poetry, an attitude which is mainly reflected in his emotional remembrances of Coole Park. "Coole Park, 1929" is his "swan song" for Coole Park, the symbolic place for Protestant aristocratic culture. In the park, great men of Gaelic literature such as Douglas Hyde, the great dramatist Synge and patrons of art Shawe Taylor and Hugh Lane once drew inspiration. Here, according to Yeats, there can be found the "pride established in humility," "a scene well set and excellent company" and only here one can find "certainty upon the dreaming air." In "Coole and Ballylee, 1931," Yeats laments the disappearance of the Protestant aristocracy by remembering standing in one wood near the lake and appreciating the swans:

> And all the rant's a mirror of my mood:
> At sudden thunder of the mounting swan

34. Here Yeats is criticizing the too strict conservatism of Catholicism represented by Saint Patrick, which can be linked to the discussion about Yeats's objection to the law of divorce. It is difficult to pinpoint what this "abstract Greek absurdity" is, but what is clear is that Yeats is against the Catholic idea of a totally masculine trinity. Such an idea is in opposition to Yeats's opinion that in nature and super-nature men, women and children (son or daughter) are all included.

I turned about and looked where branches break
The glittering reaches of the flooded lake.[35]

Coole Park was once the inspirational source for Yeats's poetry and once in the park there were always "beloved books that famous hands have found" and there were ancient marble heads and old pictures. The artists who once were under the protection of the owner of Coole Park found "content and joy," while the poet proudly claims himself to be one of "the last romantics" who chose "for theme traditional sanctity and loveliness."[36] Seemingly the poet compares Coole Park to the "Garden of Eden" in artistic creation, the owner of the park and those artists who once visited there as representatives of the arts of the Protestant aristocracy.

"Ascendency"

As discussed above, Yeats's attitude toward religion undergoes a process of change, related not only to the writer's life experience, but is also a tense reflection of the historical background and religious situation at the end of nineteenth century and the beginning of twentieth century in Ireland, reflecting at the same time Yeats's affinity to the matter of "Ascendency."

Yeats's ancestors belong to this "Ascendency" in Irish history—that which occupies the ruling position and which is normally composed of two classes: the landed clergy people (such as Yeats's paternal family) and the wealthy and powerful merchants and property owners (such as Yeats's maternal family). Since the seventeenth century, this social class had been predominant in Ireland. But by the beginning of nineteenth century, things were changing and the "Ascendency" was declining, especially for landed clergymen, with Yeats's family as a typical example. Before the Roman Church was brought to Ireland, the ancient pagan Celtic culture was in a dominant position, maintaining the Druid as the priest and as the party to hand down tradition and culture generation by generation.[37] About the fifth century, the Roman Church came to Ireland and became the major

---

35. Yeats, *Poems (New Edition)*, 244.

36. Influenced by the landing movement in nineteenth-century Ireland, Coole Park was under threat from the Catholic tenants. Soon after Lady Gregory's death, the park was confiscated and made into a flat normal land.

37. The best known Druid in the world probably is Merlin in Arthurian legends, which belong to Welsh tradition, and both Irish tradition and Welsh tradition originate from Celtic tradition.

religion. Although Protestantism was introduced to Ireland with migration from Britain to Ireland in the early sixteenth century, Protestant influence was minimal until the seventeenth century. With a series of important events in Britain such as the rise of the middle classes, the Restoration and the Glorious Revolution, the Catholic believer James II being banished from Britain in 1688, and the English Parliament welcoming Princess Mary, a Protestant, and her husband William of Orange to be their rulers, the formal place of Protestantism in England was established. Two years later, William defeated James II in a crucial battle at the Boyne near Dublin and a great many immigrants came into Ireland, most of them being Protestants; these later became the ruling class called the "Ascendency," bringing with them a form of military invasion as well as business trade and its wealth. From then on, the conflict between the Protestant ruling class (mainly landlords, clergyman and business owners) and the Catholic common people (mainly tenants, workers and servants) was in continuing motion. Until the beginning of the twentieth century, many literary works depicted the conflict in various ways.[38] In the middle of the nineteenth century the Great Famine broke out in Ireland. The famine lasted for five years and about one million people died while another two million emigrated from Ireland for survival. Because of the improper measures taken by the British government and the disastrous effect of the Great Famine, tenants asked for the redistribution of the land from the landlords and land movements began to develop. The first people to suffer losses were the landed clergymen class. Yeats's grandfather was still able to enjoy a retired life on his own land but when the time came for John Yeats to inherit the income from the family land reduced year by year until the situation become so bad that the land had to be sold. The decline of the Protestant "Ascendancy" meant the rise of the Catholic classes and in 1869 the Irish Church Act was passed, enabling Catholic believers to buy and own land.

The decline in the wealth of his family made Yeats identify more and more with lives at Coole Park, a symbol of steady income and ample environment, and with a sense of nostalgia for the ascendency that his family once enjoyed. For example, in the prelude poem in his collection *Responsibilities* (1914), the poet remembers emotionally his ancestors, calling them

---

38. For example, in 1904 an ironic paper on *A Midsummer Night's Dream* is published in *Leaders Magazine*, which shows the mutual insulting tendencies of the two sides clearly. See Bew, *Ireland*, 7–8.

"old Dublin merchant and old country scholar," who have left to the poet blood "that has not passed through any huckster's loin."

When Yeats was born, the land movement was still in its prime and the family experience of the movement made a deep impression on Yeats as he grew up. The constant moving from Dublin to Sligo to London made Yeats eager for stability and he often remembered his family's glory in past times. Yeats was also born into an age when Christianity was under serious and severe pressure and even attack, and this enabled Yeats to write without any specific religious views of his own. By the 1880s, the land movement in Ireland had reduced in momentum and the literary movement began to gain attention and influence. Yeats was one of the leaders. Even with the idea that literary revival can help in national independence, Yeats still held that politics should keep a certain distance from the arts including writing. The reaction from a Catholic audience towards his works and the works of his friends made Yeats become more and more conscious of the advantage and leadership of the Protestant aristocracy. Since his first visit to Coole Park, Yeats considered it an ideal place for artistic creation and as a symbol of Protestant aristocratic culture. The management of the Abbey Theatre had once been the center of Yeats's life and yet the reaction he saw from the Catholic audience to some events pushed him to hold a critical attitude toward Catholicism while identifying closer to his own Protestant background.

About Sir Lane's donation of pictures for a gallery, Lady Gregory wrote in her memoir that the fund raising for building the gallery and donating pictures was more difficult than expected. Citizens in Dublin thought that they had been taxed, poor people considered this kind of thing a mere luxury, and only a few wealthy people would agree to help. Later, one of these wealthy donors changed his mind and did not want to help unless the people of Ireland could prove that they wanted these pictures. This event was the reason that Yeats wrote some of his poems with such strong words as "Paudeen" and "Biddy." The publication of the poem soon provoked opposition opinion from such as newspapers as the *Irish Catholic*. These attacks on Yeats continued, one such being by his opponent Murphy writing an article in a newspaper signed with "an opinion from a Paudeen." In response, Yeats wrote the words "Paudeen's point of view it was" without any restriction of its ironic tone.[39] In the poem "September 1913" Yeats again mocked the Catholics, calling them lacking in bravery and paying

---

39. Ross, *Critical Companion*, 252.

too much attention to money making. Yeats held the idea that most Irish Catholic believers took the holy things of their religion as a round of duty which had nothing to do with life, while Irish politicians would agree that good citizens are just such a kind of people. Different from these two kinds, Yeats argued, there is another kind of Irish people who are educated and bathed in the sunshine of tradition culture, whose numbers, when the middle-class Catholics came into power, dwindled slowly. Yeats even wrote with regret that in the event of Parnell these Catholics for the first time showed that in a critical moment how shameful it would be for a person if he had no brain.[40]

As has been mentioned above, Yeats's attitude toward religion changed in the middle years of his writing career, especially after the outbreak of World War I in 1914 and the 1916 Easter Uprising, the event that makes Yeats begin to hold the idea of equality for different denominations and praise the Catholic leaders who were killed in the Uprising. This event led Yeats to reconsider his old attitude and he even wrote that in the Uprising there appears "a terrible beauty." When making annotations to his poetry, Yeats admitted that to call Catholics "Paudeen" was out of date and claimed that the 1916 Uprising would be recorded in history forever. He claims that no event apart from the 1916 Easter Uprising had moved him so much and no matter what the public opinion he would record its heroism and write poetry for the officers shot dead.[41] Such an attitude was continued in his middle-period poems such as "The Sixteen Dead" and "Rose Tree."

However, when Eire became independent Protestants continued to decline in number and Catholics became the majority possessing the controlling power. Some of the measures taken by the Catholic majority were sure to provoke uneasiness and dissatisfaction, even resentment from Yeats. With this situation of the decline of Protestants and rise of Catholics, naturally the poet would become again more nostalgic towards the "Ascendency" and it is no wonder that he would put these feelings into poetic writing. In "Are You Content," the poet commemorates his ancestors in setting up "the old stone Cross" in Sligo at Drumcliff, one of whom was a "redheaded rector in County Down" who was "a good man on a horse." Another ancestor from his mother's family, "Old William Pollexfen," is described as "that notable man." Yeats affectionately calls these ancestors "legendary men." In his autobiography, Yeats vividly describes the brave event of his

---

40. Ross, *Critical Companion*, 224–25.
41. Ross, *Critical Companion*, 88.

mother's great grandfather in giving his life for the care of patients who suffered in the Great Famine. In his mind, these ancestors were like hunters: practical, doing things with ability and fond of nature.[42] Yeats himself also experienced the land movement. In "Upon a House shaken by the Land Agitation," the poet fondly praises Coole Park again for its combination of "passion and precision," lamenting its being affected by the land movement and he sighs with great affection that if the park were to be destroyed "how should the world be luckier." In "Coole and Ballylee, 1931," the confiscation of Coole Park is compared by the poet to a "high horse" becoming "riderless," which surely provokes the association of the high horse, Ireland, losing its rider, the elegant aristocracy—in Yeats's mind, the "Ascendency."

Besides the obvious fluctuating fortunes of Protestants and Catholics and their opposition to each other for centuries, there was also influence exerted one on the other leading to a rather complicated "cultural hybridity."[43] Towards the end of the nineteenth century, there were different smaller sections of Protestants and Catholics respectively,[44] not always holding to identical doctrines or conducting similar services, and more importantly Christianity itself was under severe threat from theories of evolution and intellectual challenges.[45] This complicated cultural hybridity was also closely related to the colonial history of Ireland at that time, producing a sense of "fragmentation and discontinuity" in modern Irish peoples' mentality. This in turn prompted such a sensitive writer as Yeats to search anxiously for a kind of identity for himself, including religious identity, even though the writer may not have been a strictly religious believer.[46]

As observed in the above chapter, Yeats's obvious tendency of affinity towards the Church of Ireland (though throughout his life he was not a pious believer in any particular religious position), is not only influenced by his family's tradition, but also by the elegance and gracefulness shown by members of the Protestant aristocracy such as Lady Gregory at Coole Park. It can also be said that as a result of the interest in theories of evolution

42. Ross, *Critical Companion*, 48.

43. Bradley, *Imagining Ireland*, 2.

44. The term Protestant not only covers the state Church of Ireland but also encompasses Methodist, Baptist, and Presbyterian churches, and within the Roman Catholic Church there are schools such as the Carmelites, Jesuits, and Dominicans. See, *Yeats in Context*, 227.

45. Here the term "Christianity" is used to include all sections of religion which center on the Bible and Christ.

46. Bradley, *Imagining Ireland*, 3.

and the growth of religious free thinking at that time, and because of the influence of his father John, Yeats even as a young man, held a skeptical view on almost everything, including religion. Once, it is true, in his autobiography, Yeats wrote that in that time of doubt and uncertainty he himself was different from other people because he was a "religious" person. But in his words, the religion he found was the "Church of poetic tradition" after he was deprived of accepting one certain religious belief in childhood.[47] Because of this kind of expression in his autobiography, some people have suggested that Yeats did not believe in anything. However, as far as the author of this paper is concerned, it appears that Yeats held various beliefs or thoughts with the same weight of consideration and it seems that he did not show prejudice or favor to any particular one. Yet the fact also remains that, like Hardy ("a man caught between belief and unbelief, something between an agnostic and an atheist, who attended to the services of the Church of England to the end of his life"),[48] Yeats's works, and his poetry in particular, are so inextricably linked with religious ideas that his religious attitude is something one cannot neglect. Perhaps a fairer statement is that Yeats did not believe in any certain kind of religion or belief or thought completely and what he did was to employ the materials from all of them to create a world of his own.[49] As for the world of "the Church of poetic tradition," Yeats shows continuous, religious reflection in his poetry, sometimes with a satirical attitude toward Catholicism, sometimes with a close affinity to Protestantism and sometimes with a changing mentality.

---

47. Yeats, *Autobiographies*, 115–16.

48. Jasper, *Heaven in Ordinary*, 17.

49. A ready example of this is "cyclical theory of history." Yeats argues that two thousand years in history is a cycle—for instance, the two thousand years before Christ is a cycle which centers on classic Greek civilization and the two thousand years after Christ is another cycle which centers on Christian civilization. Each cycle has a starting point: the classic civilization cycle starts with the birth of Helen (Yeats's poem "Leda and Swan") and the Christian civilization starts with the birth of Jesus (Yeats's poem "The Second Coming"). Each cycle starts with the point and then spins in a gyre (becoming wider and wider) until it collapses to the starting point of next cycle. In Yeats's opinion, history is a cycle with two opposite gyres. See Malins and Purkins, *Preface to Yeats*; Larrissy, *W. B. Yeats*.

6

Response to Yeats
Sinking in on Truth

DAVID JASPER

READING GUANG-AN'S FASCINATING AND learned essay on Yeats and religion made me realize once again the differences between the disciplines of profound learning in different cultures and the sense of being embedded in a culture by nature before learning begins, and finally the challenge to scholarship that these differences represent. Guang-an has been studying Yeats's poetry for many years. Unlike him I am not a Yeats scholar, but I have lived, culturally, with Yeats's poetry, and to a lesser extent his plays and other writings, since I was at school in the early 1960s and they resonate with me in ways that are hard to pin down but are still deep for all that. In addition I have spent time professionally in both Eire and Northern Ireland, working in both churches and in universities. Sometimes what you "know" and feel is unexaminable, beyond the reach of footnotes and library research. The same, of course, is equally true the other way around when it comes to Chinese literature.

I remember years ago seeing a student production in the University of Iowa of Yeats's brief late play *Purgatory* (1939)—another cross cultural experience. To a good Anglican like myself, and therefore a "Protestant," of course, the doctrine of purgatory is properly forbidden—expressly condemned in the Thirty Nine Articles of Religion in the Anglican *Book of Common Prayer*. There we find these words, embedded in hundreds of years of belief—and prejudice.

> The Romish Doctrine concerning Purgatory, Pardons, Worshipping and Adoration, as well of Images as of Reliques, and also invocation of Saints, is a fond thing vainly invented, and grounded upon no warranty of Scripture, but rather repugnant to the Word of God.

Well, that is what our (or rather my) Anglican Church is supposed to teach us. And yet, for the poet and for the "nominal" Protestant Yeats, purgatory is all too real, indeed necessary, as the Old Man in the play prays, in his way, at the end in these haunting words:

> O God,
> Release my mother's soul from its dream!
> Mankind can do no more. Appease
> The misery of the living and the remorse of the dead.[1]

Purgatory is real enough in human experience, whatever the church may say about it. Like Thomas Hardy, in his different way, Yeats was a serious religious believer though yet an agnostic, a Blakean, or perhaps better, Nietzschean "Christian," obsessed with the matter of religion.

But Yeats is often a hard writer to understand and he can be obscure. I began reading his poetry after I had read, while still at school in the early 1960s, Philip Larkin's Introduction to his own earliest collection of poems, *The North Ship* (1945). (Larkin himself, I suspect, is read less today than he was when I was beginning to read poetry in those far off days.) Philip Larkin recalls a lecture given by Vernon Watkins in 1943, when "impassioned and imperative, he swamped us with Yeats."[2] Larkin admits that, when he was a young poet he tried to copy Yeats, but not particularly because he either liked or understood his verse. "I spent the next three years trying to write like Yeats, not because I liked his personality or understood his ideas but out of infatuation with his music." As a poet Yeats can be very seductive at many levels, some of them very hard to grasp. But later it was Vernon Watkins who expressed his position most succinctly, putting forward the view of another Celtic poet, Dylan Thomas: of all the poets of this century "[Thomas] thought Yeats was the greatest by miles . . . but Hardy was his favourite."[3] I understand that perfectly, and I would be hard pressed to put it more clearly.

---

1. Yeats, *Collected Plays*, 689.
2. Larkin, *North Ship*, 9.
3. Larkin, *North Ship*, 10.

That assessment has remained with me for more than fifty years now. For myself also, that is true—the greatest poet is not necessarily the one to whom you feel closest, and certainly not the one you comprehend the best. And Yeats, for me, is like that. I have always found him to be rather fascinatingly remote, and then there are those moments when he deeply addresses the soul in ways that are simply beyond understanding. And it is probably as a *religious* poet that Yeats is finally so significant; not because he is Protestant or Catholic or neither—but because in his hands language becomes an instrument which reaches most deeply into the conflicted heart of the troubled twentieth century in Ireland, into its ancient mythic depths as they welled up in the Troubles between Protestant and Catholic, between Sinn Fein and Unionists, between Irish and English. It is for this reason that my favorite book about Yeats remains T. R. Henn's *The Lonely Tower* (1950), which I initially read in 1970 as a first year undergraduate studying English literature. Not insignificantly Henn later wrote a book entitled *The Bible as Literature* (1970) which, at the time, was ground-breaking in what was to become my own academic field of literature and theology. Henn begins the Introduction to the first edition of *The Lonely Tower* with these words, which allow us almost to touch the poet himself:

> A year or two before his death I spoke with Yeats, and he asked me what quality in his work I valued most. I replied "Wisdom"; though it was indeed an imprecise word.[4]

By wisdom Henn means Yeats's capacity to reveal "stable values in thought and in mood," those elements that lie at the heart of Irish culture, possible of expression only through its ancient mythology and symbol, its history and its intertwining with religion and above all Christianity, for good and for ill.

Henn locates Yeats essentially within the poetic, Romantic tradition of William Blake, the two poets from different ages and nationalities sharing a profound sense of the enduring life and significance of the symbolic and the visionary, oddly mystical, each of them working by "a constant and cumulative historical approach to the supra-sensuous."[5] From his earliest days in Sligo Yeats had, as Guang-an has shown so clearly, an ambivalent relationship with Christianity and even more with the Protestant church of his forebears. His great-grandfather, John Yeats, had been Rector of

---

4. Henn, *Lonely Tower*, ix.
5. Henn, *Lonely Tower*, 342.

Drumcliff, near Sligo and close to Ben Bulben. His father, however, he tells us, never went to church, while Yeats admits that as a boy "I was often devout, my eyes filling with tears at the thought of God and of my own sins, but I hated church."[6] He admitted that he liked the sermon and "passages of the Apocalypse and Ecclesiastes," but church-going, on the whole, simply bored him. Nevertheless, that Yeats was a profoundly "religious" person is clear from his poetry and writings, though his religious sense is always conflicted, complex, and finally unattached. In *Explorations* (1962) he wrote "again and again with remorse, a sense of defeat, I have failed when I would write of God, written coldly and conventionally."[7]

Ultimately, for all his undogmatic roamings in myth and magic, in the kabbalistic tradition and in Indian and Arabic mysticism, Yeats finally seems closest to Nietzsche in his perversity and in his response to Christianity, though he can still write approvingly of atonement and forgiveness. But we might think only of the late, dark *Supernatural Songs*[8] in which Ribh "denounces Patrick" and "considers Christian Love insufficient":

> Then my delivered soul herself shall learn
> A darker knowledge and in hatred turn
> From every thought of God mankind has had.
> Thought is a garment and the soul's a bride
> That cannot in that trash and tinsel hide:
> Hatred of God may bring the soul to God.[9]

Christianity was but one movement of the gyres, and in Ireland riven by religious divisions between Catholic and Protestant, religion being at the very heart of its identity, Yeats ultimately sought a lonely freedom elsewhere, buried somewhere deep in the disturbing ideologies and cultural movements of the twentieth century. Yeats wrote, again with echoes of Blake in his forcefulness:

> But today the man who finds belief in God, in the soul, in immortality, growing and clarifying, is blasphemous and paradoxical. He must above all free his energies from all prepossessions not imposed by those beliefs themselves. The Fascist, the Bolshevist, seeks to turn the idea of the State into free power, and both have

---

6. Yeats, *Autobiographies*, 24.

7. Yeats, *Explorations*, 305.

8. *Supernatural Songs* is a sequence of twelve poems first published in the collection *A Full Moon in March* (1935). See Yeats, *Collected Poems*, 327–33.

9. Yeats, "Ribh Considers Christian Love Insufficient," in *Collected Poems*, 330.

reached (though the idea of the State as it is in the mind of the Bolshevist is dry and lean) some shadow of that intense energy which shall come to those of whom I speak.

When I speak of the three convictions and of the idea of the State I do not mean any metaphysical or economic theory. The belief which I call free power is free because we cannot distinguish between the things believed in and the belief; it is something forced upon us bit by bit; as it liberates our energies we sink in on truth.[10]

Yeats lived in an Ireland in which the divisions between Protestant and Catholic Christians pervaded all life and politics. His place within these divisions has been well shown by Guang-an in his chapter. But "religion" in Yeats also means something more remote and elusive than this—a deep cultural adherence which is hard to define and even harder to shake off.

---

10. Yeats, *Explorations*, 334–35.

From West to East

7

Issues in Sino-Christian Theology[1]

David Jasper

I AM VERY CONSCIOUS that the chapter that follows is the perspective of a Western Christian theologian with a very limited grasp of Chinese language and an outsider's view of the constraints upon religious belief and practice in contemporary China. This means that I do not have access to a great deal of material in Mandarin, but I do have the benefit of having taught for a period of each year in a Chinese university over the past decade, and of having friends with whom I can converse and share ideas.

The project known as "Sino-Christian theology" (*hanyu jidu shenxue*) has its origins in post-Cultural Revolution China during the 1980s, very largely though not exclusively among a group of Chinese scholars who are sometimes called "cultural Christians" (*wenhua jidutu*). This was a term probably coined by church leaders in Mainland China to refer to scholars who were mainly outside the church in China and whose studies of Christianity were pursued within the academic contexts of universities, most commonly in departments of philosophy. Sino-Christianity became finally established in academic discussion in a wider English speaking context on the publication of a volume of essays entitled *Sino-Christian Studies in China*, edited by Yang Huilin of Renmin University of China in Beijing and Daniel Yeung, the Director of the Institute of Sino-Christian Studies in Hong Kong, in 2006.[2] Among its early leading and most well known ex-

---

1. An earlier version of this chapter was published as "Issues in Sino-Christian Theology," *International Journal for the Study of the Christian Church* 19.2–3 (2019) 120–32.

2. See Yang and Yeung, *Sino-Christian Studies*; Lai and Lam, *Sino-Christian Theology*; Chow, *Theosis*.

ponents, Liu Xiaofeng was unusual inasmuch as he was formally trained in Christian theology, holding a doctorate from Basel University. Others were often academics within philosophy departments, many without church affiliation, frequently remaining unbaptized and as a result viewed with some degree of suspicion by members of Christian churches. Most typically, but by no means exclusively, "cultural Christians" have been described somewhat dryly by Jason Lam as among:

> [those] scholars [who] are not committed to the Christian faith. ... But they do not study Christianity from a cultural-nationalistic perspective: their approach is more value-neutral. Their frame of reference is shaped by the academic standards of the social and human sciences. Some of them show an appreciation of the Christian faith however.[3]

However, it is clear that no academic program can be entirely value-neutral and Sino-Christian theology has its roots firmly set in the political and cultural circumstances of contemporary China. After the events of 1949 all Christian educational institutions from schools to universities and including seminaries were closed in China. But if the study of religion remained on the agenda only to be criticized during the Cultural Revolution (1966–1976), in the period of relative openness afterwards, in the early 1980s, it was recognized that just as communism itself was rooted in Western thought, so behind that lay the doctrines of the Christian faith, as acknowledged by Marx, Engels and those who followed them.

Thus, while confessional Christianity remained controlled and confined to the churches in the "private sector," attention to Christianity and its thought flourished, at least to a degree, within the broader stream of cultural studies and within the philosophy departments of state universities. As Jason Lam admits,

> If the period of communist rule has accidentally and paradoxically created an appropriate situation for Christian study to become a formal part of the cultural and educational system of the state, this implies that the Christian faith already possessed the potential to influence the construction of modern Chinese thought in Mainland China. Liu Xiaofeng claims that this is a chance Chinese Christian intellectuals cannot afford to miss.[4]

---

3. Lai and Lam, *Sino-Christian Theology*, 22–23.
4. Lai and Lam, *Sino-Christian Theology*, 33. See also Chow, *Chinese Public Theology*.

To identify more closely such Chinese "Christian intellectuals," Lo Ping Cheung (Luo Bingxiang) of the Hong Kong Baptist University wrote an article in 1997 using the term "Chinese Apollos," which referred back to a passage in Acts 18, and the Alexandrian Jew named Apollos, who was an "eloquent man and well-versed in the scriptures," but who needed Priscilla and Aquila to explain "the Way of God to him more accurately" (Acts 18:24–28 NRSV). Lo Ping Cheung refers particularly to He Guanghu, Zhuo Xinping and Tang Yi, all scholars from the Institute on World Religions at the highly prestigious Chinese Academy of Social Sciences in Beijing. None of them was baptized.[5] In some respects the work of such scholars resembled the "cultural-linguistic alternative" in the study of Christian doctrine as proposed by George A. Lindbeck in his influential, and still important, volume *The Nature of Doctrine: Religion and Theology in a Post-liberal Age* (1984) which suggested that "religion can be viewed as a kind of cultural and/or linguistic framework or medium that shapes the entirety of life and thought."[6] The difference, however, is that Lindbeck was writing as a Professor of Theology at Yale University in a society that was deeply grounded in the traditions and forms of Christian thought, while Chinese cultural Christians study Christian theology in the context of post-Mao communist China. Chinese culture has never in its long history openly accepted Christianity to the same degree as it once accepted (and adapted) Indian Buddhism. What then, it might be asked, is the precise religious status of Sino-Christian theology, a predominantly academic and non-ecclesial phenomenon, within the larger context of the Christian tradition? What happens to Christianity as a religion when it finds itself absorbed into a cultural context so unfamiliar, perhaps even uncongenial, both ideologically and philosophically?

A key essay in response to these questions is Yang Huilin's essay "Inculturation or Contextualization: Interpretation of Christianity in Chinese Culture," first published in *Sino-Christian Studies in China* (2006), and more recently re-published and revised for Yang Huilin's book *China, Christianity, and the Question of Culture* (2014). Yang examines the process of interpretation that Christianity undergoes in the context of Chinese Confucian, and more recently Communist, culture. In past ages both Matteo Ricci in the seventeenth century and James Legge in the nineteenth century suffered

---

5. See further Lee, "'Cultural Christians' Phenomenon in China: A Hong Kong Discussion," in Lai and Lam, *Sino-Christian Theology*, 53–54.

6. Lindbeck, *Nature of Doctrine*, 33.

as Christian missionaries through the processes of inculturation into Chinese culture. As Ricci and Legge became more and more deeply absorbed in the Chinese language and culture, they were perceived by the church and by their Western colleagues as becoming too "Chinese" and were thus in danger of diluting the fundamental and "exclusive" claims of Christianity. Ultimately in such moves, adaptation to Chinese culture tended in China towards a "functional interpretation of Christianity to supplement Confucianism,"[7] Christianity accepted in China, if at all, as something like an ethical equivalent of the traditional teachings of Confucius.

After the revolution of 1911 and the establishment of the republic, the Chinese churches embraced Chinese traditional Confucian culture as a form of defense mechanism and a means of survival. In a moment we shall give some attention to Wu Leichuan's influential work *Christianity and Chinese Culture* (1936) as an articulate example of Christianity's inculturation into China, and, in many ways, a precursor of the Sino-Christian theology of the cultural Christians. In his essay Yang Huilin refers to Wu Leichuan's book and its immediate precursor, a brief article by Wu, which begins with the words, "The Chinese nation is rejuvenating! The Chinese nation is rejuvenating! The Chinese nation is rejuvenating!"[8] Christianity, it is argued by Wu in this article, should be regarded as being at the heart of the rediscovery of Chinese culture, but Yang notes that Christian theology in China seemed to have advanced little from the position of Wu Leichuan by the end of the twentieth century, quoting a 1999 essay of Liu Tingfang that "Christianity in China . . . is rich in expressions of practice, but lacks precise and accurate reasoning."[9]

In fact, Wu Leichuan and, a little earlier, Zhao Zichen[10] sought to associate the concepts of the ancient Daoist classics with Christian ideas—a process of contextualizaton that is frequently repeated in more recent Sino-Christian studies. Thus, for example, *tian ming zhi wei xing* in *The Doctrine of the Mean* was associated and compared with Genesis: "[God] breathed into his nostrils the breath of life" (Gen 2:7 NRSV).[11] The result

---

7. Yang, *China, Christianity, and the Question of Culture*, 27.

8. Yang, *China, Christianity, and the Question of Culture*, 30.

9. Liu, "What, After All: Is Christianity Spreading?," in Zhang and Zhuo, *Exploration of Indigenization*, 119.

10. See Zhao, "Christianity and Chinese Culture," in Zhang and Zhuo, *Exploration of Indigenization*, 1–17.

11. Yang, *China, Christianity, and the Question of Culture*, 31.

of such comparisons of ideas was a blunting of scriptural Christian beliefs within the broad elements of the Chinese cultural context, and ultimately a dislocation between the Christian community of *faith* in the churches of China, and the academic community of *discourse* which sustained the project of Sino-Christian theology. Although this distinction is also necessarily somewhat blurred and subject to many exceptions, it still serves to express a profound truth.

In its New Testament origins, Christianity seems to have been a counter-cultural movement, born out later in such examples as the lives and teaching of the Egyptian desert fathers and mothers of the fourth century. On the whole where churches and Christian communities have been counter-cultural in later conditions they have frequently flourished despite (or perhaps even because of) the pressures of a ruling secular culture. Such now might be the case in the numerically burgeoning contemporary Christian church, both official and unofficial, in China as it is strictly supervised or controlled by the Chinese government. The Sino-Christian theology of the cultural Christians, however, is perhaps more difficult to evaluate. While many of its exponents in Chinese universities are undoubtedly sympathetic, or even more than that, towards Christianity and its theology, it might be seen, in terms set by Yang Huilin and in a shift that extends inculturation towards contextualization,[12] as the last of three great phases of Christian theology in China. The first is that of "interpreting Jesus in terms of Buddha and Laozi" during the Nestorianism of the Tang dynasty (618–907). The second is that of "interpreting Jesus in terms of Confucianism" in the Ming and Qing dynasties (1368–1912) and beyond into the twentieth century. And the third, after the Cultural Revolution, is the period of interpreting "Jesus in terms of existential existence."[13] In the twentieth century and up until the present time, the stress has been upon the ethical role of Christianity and the perceived close links with Confucian tradition.

We should acknowledge here the profound ethical connections (as well as the distinctions) between the Christian church in China, known as the Three Self Movement (a particular compromise, it may be, with post Cultural Revolution China), and Sino-Christian theology, while recognizing the often barely theological nature of the former and the intellectualism of the latter. After Mao Zedong, Sino-Christian theology, from within the culture of Chinese academic life, has both acknowledged and to a degree

---

12. Terms established in Criveller, *Wan Ming Jidu lun*, 17–27.
13. See Yang, *China, Christianity, and the Question of Culture*, 36.

resisted the tendency towards the "ideologization" of religion, even as, since the 1970s, the "religious" character of the ideological teachings of Mao has often been noted.¹⁴ For example, both Mao Zedong and Christianity looked towards a new world and in it to new laws. Similarities have also been noted between Christianity and Mao Zedong's observation that "it is not difficult for a person to do one good thing; what is difficult is doing good things and no bad things all one's life."¹⁵ But one senses that at the heart of Sino-Christian theology there is a deeply rooted unease expressed by Yang Huilin as the "nonreligious interpretation of Christianity" from which Yang makes the distinctly uneasy comparison with Dietrich Bonhoeffer's idea of religionless Christianity.¹⁶ But coming from the deeply non-Christian culture of China this connection is difficult to sustain in a cultural context where compromise and lack of resolution are fundamental necessities, prompting Yang Huilin to end his essay slightly enigmatically with a quotation from Hans-Georg Gadamer that has been translated from German into Chinese and then from the Chinese into English concerning the interpretation of religion in different cultures: "The interpreters tend to be gradual compromises with the truths they interpret.... What else can interpretations be?"¹⁷ Is compromise, then, at the center of the whole discussion?

But Yang Huilin's reference to Bonhoeffer is not entirely without significance. In a remarkable essay entitled "The Contemporary Significance of Theological Ethics,"¹⁸ Yang draws a comparison between the two perhaps most traumatic events of the twentieth century, one in Europe and one in China: the Holocaust and the Cultural Revolution. He compares them under what he calls two "dimensions." 1: The uncontrollable fantasies of the collective unconsciousness, and 2: the frailty of our existing order and values. In each case there is an issue of who is responsible for such acts, and of the possibility of forgiveness. It is upon the latter that the conclusion of his essay concentrates. Yang writes:

> The Christian logic of love and forgiveness especially requires further expounding in the context of Chinese culture. Its premise should be "the Wholly Other," external and extrinsic to man, but

---

14. See Lardreau et al., *Christian-Marxist Dialogue*.
15. Yang, *China, Christianity, and the Question of Culture*, 40.
16. Yang, *China, Christianity, and the Question of Culture*, 43
17. Gadamer, *Zhe xue quan shi xue*, 197–98, quoted in Yang, *China, Christianity, and the Question of Culture*, 45.
18. Yang, *China, Christianity, and the Question of Culture*, 61–75.

not merely a rational choice between good and evil in actual ethical relationships or a relativized social check and balance.[19]

Yang's point is not that the "Confucian religion" of China is without a "latent motive force in ethics," but that it is nevertheless clear that "the Christian tradition is more concerned with ultimate ethical values."[20] And in both Auschwitz and the Cultural Revolution the necessary concern to establish a sense of responsibility cannot finally acknowledge forgiveness (Elie Wiesel would agree that this is here quite beyond the capacity of our humanity) except in the divine sense. Only in the divine transcendence recognized within the Christian tradition and located finally within the person of Jesus Christ, is forgiveness and reconciliation possible. Is such transcendence similarly available within the Chinese religious and philosophical tradition?

Perhaps there is indeed a sense of this possibility also in the mystical tradition of the *Tao Te Ching*, which acknowledges the decline that ensues from the loss of *Tao* (the Way) in chapter 38:

> Hence when the way was lost there was virtue; when virtue was lost there was benevolence; when benevolence was lost there was rectitude; when rectitude was lost there were the rites.[21]

What is here translated as "the rites" might best be understood as a sense of propriety or, in Yang's translation, "behaviour manners."[22] His point seems to be that within Taoist culture there is no necessary link between the religious pursuit of the Way (*Tao*) and social propriety—that is merely performing the rites of good manners which elude a proper sense of responsibility. Writing, it may be suggested, as a Sino-Christian theologian, Yang in his moving meditation upon the Holocaust and the Cultural Revolution, seems to imply the need for a sense of transcendence linked with immanence to allow for the possibility of forgiveness—or should we perhaps say salvation?

The task, then, of Sino-Christian theology, with its ultimate ethical values, within Chinese culture is indeed acknowledged, and this brings me back to the theology of Wu Leichuan as in so many ways the twentieth-century precursor of Sino-Christian theology today. We may recall Wu's

---

19. Yang, *China, Christianity, and the Question of Culture*, 73.
20. Yang, *China, Christianity, and the Question of Culture*, 73.
21. Lao Tzu, *Tao Te Ching*, 43.
22. Yang, *China, Christianity, and the Question of Culture*, 74.

startling phrase, "The Chinese nation is rejuvenating!," written shortly before the publication of his most significant book *Christianity and Chinese Culture*. What he is speaking of here is the salvation of the nation. As Sze-kar Wan, a Chinese New Testament scholar working in the United States, has written:

> Wu began with national salvation, and subjected all things, including his biblical interpretation, to that concern. For example, since it should be an individual's highest goal to sacrifice self for others, especially for the country, service for others should be regarded as the essence of religion. Religion, in turn, must serve society by reforming and transforming it; *it must therefore rid itself of the mystical and the fantastical to accomplish that purpose.*[23]

As a trained Confucian-Christian scholar Wu Leichuan was always suspicious of the theology and principles of biblical interpretation of Western missionaries in China. For him, as for many modern Chinese scholars in Christian theology of his time and since, "soteriology could only mean national salvation."[24] At the heart of such Chinese Christian theology lies a Christology that regards Jesus's task and mission as to reconstruct society and within it to remake the individual.[25] In short, Jesus emerges as a Confucian sage from the pages of the gospels read through the lens of Confucian ethics and philosophy, and Grace Hui Liang is led to conclude: "Wu's biblical hermeneutics thus failed to make clear the contribution Christianity could bring to China which Confucianism could not provide."[26] Christian theology then, it would seem, becomes little more than an addendum to Confucian thought.

As Chloë Starr has made clear in her recent fine book *Chinese Theology* (2016), Wu's concept of the Messiah and the Kingdom of Heaven was constructed around the rebuilding of the Chinese nation and there was little ecclesial in his Christian thinking or theology. Starr suggests:

---

23. Wan, "Six Competing Tensions: A Search for May Fourth Biblical Hermeneutics," in Starr, *Reading Christian Scriptures in China*, 107 (emphasis added).

24. Liang, "Interpreting the Lord's Prayer for a Confucian-Christian Perspective: Wu Leichuan's Practice and Contribution to Chinese Biblical Hermeneutics," in Starr, *Reading Christian Scriptures in China*, 124.

25. Wu, "Jesus as I Know Him," 77.

26. Liang in Starr, *Reading Christian Scriptures in China*, 128.

> If there was no need for miracles in the kingdom of the Republican or Nationalist China, *the church was not essential to its construction,* either.[27]

For Wu, the Kingdom of Heaven is the key metaphor in Christianity and it is perceived fundamentally in terms of social reform, almost entirely lacking in any eschatological or ecclesial dimension. His understanding of the Trinity connects the Holy Spirit with Confucian teaching on *ren* (universal love or benevolence), even going so far as to suggest that they are simply "different names for the same reality,"[28] and Wu's teaching on Jesus and the Kingdom of Heaven are taken almost entirely from Confucian ideas.

I have given some attention to Wu Leichuan and his writings in China during the Republican period in the 1930s, as they clearly relate to many of the characteristics of the more recent, post-Cultural Revolution, project of Sino-Christian theology. That too is primarily an intellectual, non-ecclesial movement, largely set apart from the life of the Christian church in China, and rooted in the cultural context of contemporary university and academic life. This observation is not intended to be cynical, but rather to extend the difficult questions of the contextualization of Christianity in Chinese culture, both ancient and modern, and even the debated understanding of the nature of "religion" itself. Ancient Chinese philosophy and religious thought do not offer the same categories and concepts, not least that of transcendence, as lie within the Greek philosophical roots of Western Christian theology, making it more comprehensible why Nestorianism[29] was able to take some root in the seventh century[30] and Christology was largely regarded within the concept of the Confucian sage in the early part of the twentieth century.

The writings (I am limited, of course, to those published in English) and theology of more recent Sino-Christian theologians become more readily understandable against this background. In Pan-chiu Lai and Jason Lam's edited volume on *Sino-Christian Theology: A Theological Qua Cultural Movement in Contemporary China* (2010), an essay by the Chinese New

---

27. Starr, *Chinese Theology*, 152 (emphasis added).

28. Wu, *Christianity and Chinese Culture*, 38.

29. This term is notoriously difficult to pin down, but by the later fifth century in the West was applied to upholders of a strict Antiochene Christology by all their opponents. See *Oxford Dictionary of the Christian Church*, 1145–46.

30. See Whyte, *Unfinished Encounter*, 33–40.

Testament scholar, now teaching in the USA, Yeo Khiok-Khng, is entitled "Messianic Predestination in Romans 8 and Classical Confucianism."[31] This is hermeneutically more sophisticated than the writings of Wu Leichuan, but it remains very similar in terms of its understanding of Messiahship and the Kingdom. Yeo Khiok-Khng begins his essay with these words:

> [This] experimental essay seeks to use an inter-subjective hermeneutic to read the texts of Paul and Confucius intertextually. The reading is concerned with crossing borders and fusing horizons in cross-cultural interpretation. The paper will read Paul's messianic (Christological) predestination language using the lens of the Confucian millennial understanding of *Datong* (Great Togetherness).[32]

There is certainly here a more intercultural, dialogical tone together with a post-Kristevan sense of intertextuality, but one is left again with a sense that the Confucian foundations remain essentially undisturbed and the language of the Christian "supplement" still lingers. Yeo Khiok-Khng admits to his "Confucianist assumptions of history,"[33] significantly noting in his conclusion that he finds that "Paul's eschatological definition of the goal (the end) of history from the future *supplements* my Confucianist retrieval reading of history from the past golden age."[34]

Religious shifts, and the even the meaning of religion, between cultures are never simple or straightforward. During the Jesuit mission to China of 1583–1721, Matteo Ricci identified closely with the culture of Chinese literati in Beijing, though his welcome was also balanced by a deep suspicion among many Chinese intellectuals as to his intentions. But the really fatal opposition to Ricci and the Jesuit mission came from the papacy and Rome itself, fearing the dilution of the fundamentals of Christianity in an alien culture. On March 26, 1693, Charles Maigrot, the Vicar-Apostolic in Fujian, forbade rites honoring ancestors (which Ricci himself viewed as commemorative and not a form of worship) and the use of the terms *Tian* and *Shangdi* for God.[35] Although the Emperor was willing to negotiate, the

---

31. Lai and Lam, *Sino-Christian Theology*, 179–201.
32. Lai and Lam, *Sino-Christian Theology*, 179.
33. Lai and Lam, *Sino-Christian Theology*, 181.
34. Lai and Lam, *Sino-Christian Theology*, 200 (emphasis added).
35. See Whyte, *Unfinished Encounter*, 70; Ebrey, *Cambridge Illustrated History of China*, 225.

Papal Bull *Ex Illa Die* of 1715 finally brought the Jesuit mission to a close. The Vatican did not reverse its ruling until 1939.

Sino-Christian theology, then, is a Chinese venture born out of a complex and lasting intercultural context. The Christian exclusivity that ended the work of Matteo Ricci was experienced again by perhaps the best known Western missionary to China of the nineteenth century, James Legge (1815–1897), later the first professor of Chinese Literature and Language in Oxford. Legge was a strong advocate for the term *Shangdi* as the most appropriate for the scriptural and Christian word God.[36] In 1877, the Shanghai Missionary Conference effectively brought Legge's long years as a missionary in China (or more precisely Hong Kong) to an end as the "heretic" Legge was understood as promoting Confucianism as a religion and Confucius himself was being promoted as more or less on a par with the Hebrew prophets.[37] In the official proceedings of the Shanghai Conference, at which Legge was not present, we read that "a resolution proposed by Rev. S. L. Baldwin to omit [Legge's] essay and discussion on Confucianism from the published record" was passed "without dissenting voice."[38] Legge was, by training and inclination, an intellectual and a scholar, with an increasingly uneasy relationship to his church, to which he nevertheless remained faithful to the end. But his true vocation was found in Oxford, as a university professor.

Thus it is perhaps not entirely surprising that James Legge is better remembered today among Chinese scholars in Chinese universities than he is in either Oxford or his native Scotland. In recent years, Sino-Christian theology and scholars like Yang Huilin (who actually first introduced me to the writings of Legge) have been attracted to the project known as "Scriptural Reasoning" in the promotion of Christian theology and intercultural religious study in China. Yang describes Scriptural Reasoning simply and clearly:

36. James Legge was at the heart of what in the nineteenth century was known as the Term Question—whether there is an appropriate Chinese word for God and what it should be.

37. In his lectures given in London in 1880 and published as *Religions in China: Confucianism and Taoism Described and Compared with Christianity*, Legge more or less overtly links Confucius with Hebrews 1:1–2: "God, who at sundry times and in divers manners spake in time past to the fathers by the prophets." In making this link between the Hebrew prophetic tradition and the writings of Confucius, Legge was also anticipating Karl Jaspers's concept of the Axial Age of the global flourishing of cultures ca. 600–300 BCE.

38. *Records*, 15, quoted in Girardot, *Victorian Translation of China*, 216.

The term "scriptural reasoning," originating from the term "textual reasoning," was first introduced in the early 1990s by a group of Jewish scholars who followed the examples of Hermann Cohen, Martin Buber, and Emmanuel Levinas, and attempted to re-read the Christian Bible and the Jewish Tanakh and later on also the Muslim Quran, from the perspective of transculturalism and comparative studies.[39]

Immediately evident is the academic quality of Yang's definition—the remark of a scholar who is concerned with textual interpretation, with scholarly predecessors and with dialogical exercises in transcultural reading. It is no accident that the essay that precedes this remark in Yang's book is concerned with the work of James Legge. And the Sino-Christian theological unease that ended Legge's years as a missionary in China remains today among the Chinese scholars who continue to study his legacy as one of the greatest translators of the Chinese Classics and Confucianism into English and yet also a promoter, as a missionary, of Christianity and its theology.

In a book which I recently co-edited with Geng Youzhuang and Wang Hai, two Chinese colleagues from Beijing, entitled *A Poetics of Translation: Between Chinese and English Literature* (2016),[40] there is an essay by a young Chinese scholar from Renmin University of China, Zhao Jing, entitled "A Study of the 'Preface' and 'Introduction' to James Legge's *The Texts of Taoism*."[41] The final few pages of this essay, concerned with Christianity and "comparative studies," are slightly uneasy and even hesitant in their tone. That is not intended to be a criticism, for perhaps this is necessarily the case. Zhao is clear that Legge never abandons his sense of the priority of Christianity, "while nevertheless the three Chinese religions[42] (*san jiao*, 'three teaching systems') can give another lesson *less pharisaical*."[43] On the other hand Zhao clearly shows the limits of Legge's understanding of Taoism even while he shared some of its most profound principles such as "deep predilections for a Divine order or fixed imperial design and traditional moral civility."[44] But Legge's affinity with many of these principles has

---

39. Yang, *China, Christianity, and the Question of Culture*, 163.
40. Later also published in Chinese.
41. Jasper et al., *Poetics of Translation*, 93–111.
42. Taoism, Buddhism, and Confucianism.
43. Zhao in Jasper et al., *Poetics of Translation*, 108 (emphasis added).
44. Girardot, *Victorian Translation of China*, 438.

been attributed by the American Legge scholar Lauren Pfister to his academic rootedness, established while he was a student at Aberdeen University, in the Scottish Enlightenment[45]—a recognition of apparent similarities between cultures that might often cloud deep differences.

Legge clearly appeals to Chinese scholars in contemporary Sino-Christian theology for a number of reasons, not least his profoundly academic sense of theology and religion. Nevertheless, and at the same time, the deep fissures in the project are illuminated by the comparison. Just as Legge, like Matteo Ricci before him, remained solidly Christian and Western in his thinking, his immersion in Chinese thought and culture was the cause of suspicion, more from his fellow Protestant European missionaries than from China itself. So Chinese scholars of Sino-Christian theology, though often learned in Western thought and theology as well as intercultural projects such as "Scriptural Reasoning" (which originated in the USA), and holding in respect the learned tradition of Christianity, yet remain embedded in Chinese and Confucian values, ethics and forms of thought. In academic contexts, comparative studies are certainly to be encouraged as cultures and traditions seek to address one another. But the lack of an ecclesial context and practicing faith-based community within the Chinese church must place questions as to what kind of "Christian" theology can emerge in Sino-Christian theology from an essentially academic context, as well as to the nature of how these two contexts—the church and the academy in China—finally relate to one another.

---

45. Pfister, *Striving*.

8

Response to Issues in Sino-Christian Theology

Ou Guang-an

BEING ALMOST A COMPLETE outsider in the field of Christian theology, I am somewhat at a loss as to how to begin to respond to David's acute perception, only this time it is the perception of the history, development and current problematic situation of Sino-Christian theology. At the same time being an outsider also has some sort of advantage, that is, one can look at something from an out-of-the-circle perspective, as a famous Chinese short poem by Bian Zhilin suggests: "You are standing on the bridge looking at views, / The person looking at views from a window is looking at you. / Bright moonshine decorates your window, / While you decorate someone's dream."[1] Thus, there is the case for my reading of David's essay on Sino-Christian theology. I am not qualified to discuss in theological detail what is happening inside the field of Sino-Christian theology, to quote René Wellek and Austin Warren from the *Theory of Literature* (1949), the "intrinsic study," but I may have some reflection to offer on some "outside" factors of the theology in general, or the "extrinsic study." And one such extrinsic factor which interests me is the investigation on the possible reason that contemporary Sino-Christian theological studies are pursued most commonly in departments of philosophy in various Chinese universities or academic institutions.

---

1. Bian Zhilin, *New Collection*, 13.

The reasons on the surface are not difficult to find. On one hand, in the modern Chinese academic context, theological studies are normally considered as belonging to the broader field of "religious studies" and in most academic institutions there is no specific department of religious studies. Rather religious studies is situated within the philosophy department of a university or college. On the other hand, within the church there probably is not enough staff who can both hold an ecclesiastical position and enjoy intellectual or academic influence. However, I would like to argue about this from another perspective, that is, the subtle interplay between the neglected role of philosophical studies and the inseparability of literature, history and philosophy within the Chinese tradition.

The Chinese sense of philosophy and the forming of philosophical concepts within the ancient traditions come much later than those of literature and history, and some researchers would argue that the Chinese understanding of philosophy derives ultimately from Indian influence. As far as disciplines are concerned, philosophy is invariably the last that is talked about, written about and discussed in Chinese traditional culture, understood in its broadest sense. Synchronically the traditional ancient Chinese texts are categorized into four types: classics (especially Confucian classics), historic records, records of different schools of thoughts and collections of poetry. Among these four categories, the branch that philosophy is closest to is the third and even in this third category not all of the works can be defined as philosophical works. Diachronically, the numbers of literary and historical works in Chinese history significantly outnumber those of philosophical works. We only have to take a brief glimpse at Chinese traditional writings to know that in the time of the Tang Dynasty the dominant writing was poetry, in the Song Dynasty it was *ci* (a variation of poetry, or lyrical poetry), in the Yuan Dynasty it was *qu* (a type of verse) and, finally, in the Ming and Qing Dynasties it was fiction and the novel. With each period of historical writing there have appeared volumes and volumes of historical records on previous dynasties. As for philosophical writing, it is either scattered in various other writings or entirely absent for some periods. When it comes to academic writing, various periods in ancient Chinese history witnessed some writing in appreciation of poetry or lyrical poetry such as *Cang Lang's Discussion on Poetry* by Yan Yu around the 1230s, and so on. However, what can be claimed as authentic academic writing on philosophy is quite sparse and systemic research on the discipline of philosophy came only as late as the early twentieth century with the publication of Hu

Shi's *Outline of Chinese History of Philosophy* (1919) as the landmark event. Another influential work of a similar stature is Feng Youlan's *Brief History of Chinese Philosophy* (1948), published in the United States by Macmillan, a collection of his lectures on Chinese philosophy history given at the University of Pennsylvania. In the modern Chinese academic context, with the introduction of an education system that is drawn mainly from western academic models, a department of philosophy is normally an independent institute like that of history and literature and it is usually combined with the discipline of languages. Also, the absence of any religion being formally recognized as a primary way of thinking and practice in any dynasty in ancient Chinese history gives rise to the result that the study of religion is subordinated to the broad study of philosophy in the modern Chinese academic context.

In traditional Chinese culture, understood in its broadest sense, the marginal position of philosophy is clear enough. However, from another perspective, philosophy, or at least philosophical observations took place quite often, mainly scattered in other forms of writing as literature and history. Thus one often heard the saying, almost a cliché, that "literature, history and philosophy are in one integrated family." This does bear some truth in it, especially for such classical works as the *Analects* or the *Historical Records*. In Book XI, Chapter XXV of the *Analects*, Confucius the Master asked his disciples about their wishes and one of them Zeng Dian answered:

> In this, the last month of spring, with the dress of the season all complete, along with five or six young men who have assumed the cap, and six or seven boys, I would wash in the I [a river] enjoy the breeze among the rain altars, and return home singing." The Master heaved a sigh and said, "I give my approval to Tien (Zeng Dian).[2]

Before Zeng Dian, several other disciples had expressed their wishes, mostly about becoming statesmen, managing states of different sizes. So when Zeng Dian stated his answer, which was in distinct contrast to others, the dramatic moment came when the Master "heaved a sigh" and said he would agree with Zeng Dian. The historical context of the passage, compared to literary narration, seems the more obvious because in Confucius's time (the period of Spring and Autumn, roughly from the eighth to the fifth century BCE) different rulers controlled different parts of China and

2. Confucius, *Confucian Analects* [Legge], 153.

warfare was frequent. Even Confucius himself had to flee for safety from time to time. Thus it is no wonder that the majority of his disciples on this occasion would choose to manage the affairs of state. But with that meaningful action of heaving a sigh comes the complexity of Confucius's thought. For one thing, he actively proposed that one should make great efforts in "entering into the world," that is, talking less of eccentricities or baseless things and shouldering more responsibility in the management of a state with benevolence. This is quite opposite to the Daoist submissiveness to whatever happens to one, an attitude of "walking out of the world (worldly affairs)." For another thing, after making so many endeavors in publicizing his idea in various states, when Confucius saw that the states were still in conflict with one another the Master probably revealed his frustration and even hopelessness by showing such an "out-of-the-world-affair" attitude in agreeing with Zeng Dian.

The formation of the *Analects* took place in what the German thinker Karl Theodor Jaspers once called the Axial Age and a further investigation of classical works in such an age would reveal that the integrated nature of literature, history and philosophy did not only conform to Confucian canons but probably also to a large degree to the Hellenic and Hebrew traditions. And probably this is another reason that scholars in Sino-Christian theology could identify with such methodologies as "Scriptural Reasoning," again, in its broadest sense.

One of Aesop's fables goes like this:

> A waggoner was driving his team along a muddy lane with a full load behind them, when the wheels of his waggon sank so deep in the mire that no efforts of his horses could move them. As he stood there, looking helplessly on, and calling loudly at intervals upon Hercules for assistance, the god himself appeared, and said to him, "Put your shoulder to the wheel, man, and goad on your horses, and then you may call on Hercules to assist you. If you won't lift a finger to help yourself, you can't expect Hercules or any one else to come to your aid."[3]

The philosophical significance of this fable is easy to discern. Indeed the English saying "God helps those that help themselves" is derived from this very fable. The literary elements are also not so difficult to understand; the beginning (the Waggoner's driving a heavy load along a very muddy way), the development (his wagon becomes caught deep in the mire), and

3. Aesop, *Aesop's Fables*, 89.

the climax (the Waggoner's asking for help from Hercules and Hercules's refusal). The historical and cultural origins of the fable are clear enough—in the situation of a common trade such as a waggoner in ancient Greece, and, the background in the formation of Greek mythology and fable.

In the Hebrew tradition, such origins would also seem apparent, though probably with a more religious overtone. For instance, the Babel narrative runs thus:

> And the whole earth was of one language, and of one speech. And it came to pass, as they journeyed from the east, that they found a plain in the land of Shinar; and they dwelt there And they said one to another, Go to, let us make brick, and burn them thoroughly. And they had brick for stone, and slime had they for mortar. And they said, Go to, let us build us a city and a tower, whose top may reach unto heaven; and let us make us a name, lest we be scattered abroad upon the face of the whole earth. And the LORD came down to see the city and the tower, which the children of men builded. And the LORD said, Behold, the people is one, and they have all one language; and this they begin to do; and now nothing will be restrained from them, which they have imagined to do. Go to, let us go down, and there confound their language, that they may not understand one another's speech. So the LORD scattered them abroad from hence, upon the face of all the earth: and they left off to build the city. Therefore is the name of it called Babel; because the LORD did there confound the language of all the earth: and from thence did the LORD scatter them abroad upon the face of all the earth. (Gen 11:1–9 KJV)[4]

Here there is cause (people want to build a tower to reach into heaven) and effect (they are scattered all over the earth) and there is also in the narrative the beginning (people decide to make a name), the development (they build the tower), the climax (God decides to interfere) and the ending (people are scattered). One of the historical investigations into this narrative could be into the beginnings of different languages in the primitive stage of civilizations. The theological significance can be found in many volumes of writings and for an outsider to theology such as myself at least some observations can be made such as the subtle relationship between the Creator and the created, the complexity of the authority of the Lord and the people's challenge to this authority and so on. Thus, after Babel, how we can

---

4. The intentional use of the Authorized Version here is to keep its classical tone as in the *Analects* and *Aesop's Fables*.

communicate at all requires our detailed attention. Thus different cultures struggle with the origins of religious thinking—and the Chinese have their own way of addressing the nature of biblical—and Christian—theology.

9

Towards a Reading of Lu Xun

David Jasper

Lu Xun's abandonment of his medical studies in Japan and his embracing of a literary vocation was rooted in the moment, so he tells us in his Preface to his short story collection *Outcry* (1923), when he famously witnessed a group of Chinese people standing by apathetically, watching the "grand spectacle" of a Chinese prisoner who had served as a spy for the Russians about to be decapitated by a Japanese soldier. Seeing their apathy he turned, he tells us, from a concern for diseases of the body to the question of the disease of the soul. From this moment he turned his attention from the study of medicine to the practice of literature:

> Citizens of an ignorant and weak nation, no matter how healthy and sturdy their bodies can serve as nothing more than subject matter for or spectators of meaningless public displays. That many of them die of disease is not, necessarily, something unfortunate. Our most important mission lies in transforming their spirits, and at the time I felt that the best way to transform their spirits was, of course, through literature, and so I wanted to promote a literary movement.[1]

At this time (1906), Lu Xun and a few colleagues expressed their concern to embark on this project by reviving the classics of Chinese literature through a new journal they called *Vita Nova* (*New Life*).

This story is well enough known in modern Chinese literary history, but it begs the question as to what precisely we might understand by the idea

---

1. Lu Xun, *Jottings under Lamplight*, 21.

here of "spirit," particularly in a writer who not infrequently protests that he knows nothing about religion at all. But at the same time Lu Xun must have been familiar with the then popular translations of Western literature into Chinese by Lin Shu (1852–1924)—a man who knew no foreign languages—not least Lin's famed 1905 translation of Harriet Beecher Stowe's novel *Uncle Tom's Cabin* which renders the familiar song of the angels to the shepherds, "Peace on earth, good will to men" (Luke 2:14) as "the *qi* of Dao," while the Christian idea of "that kingdom which God will set up" becomes, without eschatological resonance, "world union" (*shijie datong*).[2] In Lin Shu, Confucian values control Western religious (and usually Christian) terms and ideas. Lu Xun's own attitude towards Confucius and traditional Chinese values was more ambivalent, but the issue of "spirituality" remains pertinent as his writings—mainly short stories and essays—became part of world literature in the twentieth century.

At the same time Lu Xun's high reputation in China was simultaneously both enhanced and compromised by his acceptance under Mao Zedong as a "revolutionary paragon."[3] On the anniversary of Lu Xun's death, on 19 October 1937, Mao Zedong gave a speech which raised the writer to the status of "a Chinese sage of the first order," on a level, indeed, with the Confucius of the feudal age. It was an accolade that profoundly compromises the delicate literary nuances of the writer himself and his actual cultural and artistic achievement. But Lu Xun's place within Chinese history as well as literature cannot be insignificant. My readings of some of his short stories and essays that follow are by a non-Chinese speaking critic. I am well aware that reading them in English translations misses the subtleties and frequent historical, cultural and geographical references of Lu Xun's original writing and achievements, not least those in *baihua*—or the language of common people. But if we recognize Lu Xun as a writer of international status then, like others, he must take his chance in translation, a radically iconoclastic figure as well as one rooted in his Chinese past as well as its present. In his recent study of "comparative" to "world literature" (written in English), the distinguished contemporary Chinese critic Zhang Longxi has pointed out that the standard textbook *Norton Anthology of World Literature* more or less excluded non-Western works until its "expanded" edition of 1995, while in the early twentieth century, Lu Xun and others of the May Fourth new culture movement in China were including classical Chinese fiction

2. Der-Wei Wang, "Chinese Literature," 535.
3. Davies, *Lu Xun's Revolution*, 6.

such as the great eighteenth-century novel *A Dream of Red Mansions* (*Hong Lou Meng*), sometimes known as *The Story of the Stone*, in the pantheon of world literature.[4]

Further to this, Lu Xun and his brother Zhou Zuoren published during their time in Japan two collections of *Fictions from Abroad* to bring to a Chinese readership, through literal translations, a sense of the suffering and oppressions of other nations. Commercially a failure and influenced by Russia's White Revolution of 1905, these translations sought to bring China into an international cultural and literary arena in which literature was perceived as a powerful social and political tool, a spiritual medicine for the people, we might say.

But perhaps more than a writer of short fictions, Lu Xun was above all an essayist, well versed in ancient Chinese literary forms, yet endlessly experimental, allusive, contradictory, often deeply layered and bitingly caustic. That tone comes through even in English translation. Yet born out of, and living in, a world of violence and social change, these brief literary fragments are extremely difficult to "hear" in translation.

Let me begin with Lu Xun's essay on one of his own most familiar fictional writings, "How *The True Story of Ah-Q* Came About" (1926).[5] When I first read this novella, entitled *The Real Story of Ah-Q* in a recent English translation by Julia Lovell, I was aware, through a sense of readerly unsettlement, of the truth of the translator's comment on its narrator and narrative form, that "our condescending biographer, we realize, is a thoroughly compromised man who slips between the various worlds that he parodies."[6] The slippages in narrative distance—the unreliable narrator at one moment a distant observer among the villages and yet in the next moment inside Ah-Q's very thought processes—are disconcerting and at times disorienting. But his essay on how the story came about is equally problematic, both affirming and yet not affirming:

> Whether Ah-Q really wanted to be a revolutionary, or suppose that he did become a revolutionary, whether he seems to be two different personalities are things we shall leave aside for the moment.[7]

---

4. Zhang Longxi, *From Comparison to World Literature*, 174–75.
5. Lu Xun, *Jottings under Lamplight*, 36–44.
6. Lovell, "Introduction," xxiii.
7. Lu Xun, *Jottings under Lamplight*, 37.

Lu Xun is a writer, we might say, who speaks most loudly when he fails to speak, one who disarmingly suggests to his reader that "I neither have anything to say nor anything I wish to write." And yet he insistently does speak and write, even to the very end of his life. He became, he admits, tired of the character of Ah-Q and wanted him "finished off," though he admits that the details of this he has simply forgotten, its memory "no longer very clear." All writers of fiction know, of course, that characters of fiction finally write themselves, but this should not exonerate the writer from responsibility for what happens to them or what they are. And so it is with the end, and the death, of Ah-Q, his "grande finale" which Lu Xun almost seems to link with his own end and his ultimate reputation, whatever that might be. But the same might be said of all of us. In what sense can we choose our end and to what extent are we responsible for what people will finally think of us? Finally, the writer disappears, refusing to give anything away: Lu Xun states—"Ah-Q, naturally, could have had any number of other outcomes, but I know nothing about them."[8]

Here is the end of *The Real Story of Ah-Q*,[9] written in December 1921, the reader drawn into the ogling, bestial crowd at Ah-Q's execution:

> Public opinion in Weizhuang was undivided: of course Ah-Q was a villain—he wouldn't have been shot otherwise. The verdict in town was more ambivalent: death by firing squad, the majority of them felt, wasn't a patch on decapitation. And the condemned had been a miserable specimen. In that whole extended tour around the streets, he hadn't managed to choke out a single line of opera; they had followed him for nothing.[10]

Such a manic crowd is not unknown elsewhere in world literature. The ending of Patrick Süskind's *Perfume* (1985) and its crowd, comes to mind. In a time of violence and revolution, the narrator of Lu Xun's story catches perfectly the self-justifications and the barely disguised obscenity of public opinion, catching also the reader off guard, surprised by sin. Are *we*, you and I, then, included in the condemnation—and Lu Xun himself? Possibly. He once suggested, rather evasively, that "I wrote *The Real Story* with the intention of exposing the weakness of my fellow citizens—I did not specify whether or not I myself was included therein."[11]

8. Lu Xun, *Jottings under Lamplight*, 42.
9. Even the title in English is slippery—is this the *real* story or the *true* story of Ah-Q?
10. Lu Xun, *Real Story*, 123.
11. Lu Xun, quoted in Liu, *Translingual Practice*, 70.

Satirical writing penned at a time of cultural upheaval is written quite deliberately so that it is never easy to pin it down, most especially when it comes from the pen of a writer like Lu Xun who has mastery of a literary tradition that is embedded in, for someone like myself, an outsider, a mysterious intellectual culture and language that here is at once employed and deconstructed. Adopted into the revolutionary cause by Mao Zedong, Lu Xun is, at the same time, even more revolutionary as a writer, and is as such a master of disguise and ambivalence. The last thing he wants as a writer is to become "a kind of respectable monument,"[12] ironically becoming monumental in his reputation by studied disrespect in the service of freedom. Language is both an instrument of freedom and an expression, *ad absurdum*, of the self-defeating purposes of revolution. In Lu Xun's aphorism written in response to the violence of 1927 in China, "Revolution; revolutionize the revolution; revolutionize the revolutionized revolution; revolutionize . . . (geming gegeming gegegeming, gege),"[13] language parodies the thing—and the sound of the machine gun (in the Chinese), as it were outguns the gun's definitiveness.

A characteristic brief essay of 1925 is entitled "This is What I Meant."[14] It is a reactive piece, written in response to a letter by Zhao Xueyang and an accusation that Lu Xun had read a great deal of Chinese literature but was unwilling to encourage other people to read it. Lu Xun's advice is clear, but what he *means* by this advice is much more elusive. He advises young Chinese people: "read fewer Chinese books—if at all—and read more foreign books."[15] He then launches into a kind of parable by way of explanation. He describes his own addiction to alcohol, which at first he found rather comforting. Lu Xun was indeed a heavy drinker and smoker. His drinking is likened to his reading of Chinese literature. "Nowadays I sometimes abstain and sometimes still drink, just like I still leaf through some Chinese books." The parallel drawn between drinking and Chinese literature is sharp, but its "meaning" is not immediately apparent. It remains deliberately unexplained. Lu Xun continues with two further images:

> Even if I was suffering from smallpox, I would not on that account be opposed to cowpox; even if I owned a coffin shop, I would not sing the praises of the plague.

12. Lu Xun, quoted in Davies, *Lu Xun's Revolution*, 170.
13. Lu Xun, quoted in Davies, *Lu Xun's Revolution*, 63.
14. Lu Xun, *Jottings*, 197–98.
15. Lu Xun, *Jottings*, 197.

That is pretty much what I meant.[16]

But what *did* he mean? Of course, in a sense, one gets the point: the owner of the coffin shop is the preserver of the moribund Chinese tradition, but he does not invite more customers by invoking the aid of the plague. He will not kill off that which sustains and endorses the tradition. So—what does he mean?

The brief essay concludes with something apparently completely unrelated. "Let me add a statement on an unrelated matter while I am at it."[17] The detour is an explanatory note on an earlier essay by Lu Xun, "Warriors and Flies," which ends with an irritated swipe at all critics, who are "hardly annoying enough to qualify as 'flies.'" The essay concludes with the words: "I mention all of this here merely to avoid any misunderstandings."[18] In short, we are left thinking we know precisely what Lu Xun means, yet at the same time uncomfortably aware that we are not quite sure how to decode his images and metaphors. We know but do not know, and yet we are provoked into thought. Lu Xun's satirical tone, his irony and evasions, his guarded understatements and his abrupt changes and alterations in voice are the very stuff of literature, though his culture and his language are very hard for an outsider to Chinese language and culture to "hear" and judge. Like all great writers he voices the dilemma of his age and time in a China that was still deeply traditional and yet riven by the incursions of modernity. As the critic David Der-Wei Wang, a professor of Chinese literature at Harvard University, has expressed it: "In literary practice, what makes writers like Lu Xun . . . outstanding is that their works bear witness to the treacherous terms of articulating modernity under the shadow of tradition."[19]

That is a familiar dilemma in more walks of life than that of the literary (not least the religious), but it is perhaps all the more acute in early twentieth-century China that was still culturally remote from the Eurocentrism of most study of comparative literature, and yet was emerging from an ancient and entrenched cultural system with traumatic and often violent haste, imposed upon by Marxist ideological principles that were originally articulated under very different, distant, and Western historical circumstances.

16. Lu Xun, *Jottings*, 198.
17. Lu Xun, *Jottings*, 198.
18. Lu Xun, *Jottings*, 198.
19. Der-Wei Wang, "Chinese Literature," 559.

What then of Lu Xun the story-teller, the self-appointed healer of the spiritual ills of China? Exposing the weakness of his fellow citizens, Lu Xun speaks in a literary voice that is biting, ambiguous, demanding and humane. In the words of his translator Julia Lovell:

> Lu Xun's vocational epiphany, with its powerful evocation of the lone, enlightened intellectual pledging to transform the benighted Chinese masses, was mired in the uncertainties of this new nationalist vision: in a combination of high-minded contempt and patriotic sympathy that he would later shape in a fictional oeuvre of ingenious moral ambiguity.[20]

I avoid comment on the first and one of his best-known stories, "Diary of a Madman" with its parabolic reference to its Russian predecessor. Instead I want to consider a brief fragment of a story written in July, 1920 entitled "A Minor Incident."[21] It is a mere three pages long.

The narrator—is it actually Lu Xun himself?—is clearly well-to-do, a citizen who has lived in Beijing for six years after the revolutionary upheavals of 1911 that finally brought an end to the Qing Dynasty, and he is unimpressed by great national events except insofar as they induce in him a feeling of depression and contempt for his fellow citizens. But he is jolted out of his complacency by a small incident of a kind that is by no means unusual in Beijing or indeed any other great city—a little street accident involving the rickshaw in which he is travelling which inadvertently knocks an elderly, poor woman down. It is not the rickshaw runner's fault, for he swerved to avoid the old woman, but her clothes had caught in his rickshaw. The old woman is lying on the ground, probably not seriously hurt, and the narrator feels only irritation as his runner who, by staying to help the old woman, risks getting himself into trouble.

The rickshaw runner helps the old woman to her feet, even helping her towards a nearby police station, at great risk to himself who may well be accused of knocking her over. The narrator is cross, perhaps afraid, but then is overcome by a paralysis that is both physical and mental. "It seemed to bear down on me, pressing out the petty selfishness concealed beneath my fur coat."[22] He walks towards a policeman, hands him some coins and walks away, trying to distance himself from the event and a series of questions forming in his mind:

20. Lovell, "Introduction," xvii.
21. Lu Xun, *Real Story*, 53–55.
22. Lu Xun, *Real Story*, 54.

> As I walked along, I was thinking—almost afraid I would turn my thoughts on myself. None of it had anything to do with me; so what had I meant by that handful of coins? Was it a reward? Did I have the right to pass such judgement? I could not answer my own questions.

To a Western, Christian reader like myself, the story has inevitable overtones of the parable of the Good Samaritan (Luke 10:30–37), or that parable's endless perverted revisions in Malcolm Lowry's great tragic novel *Under the Volcano* (1947). Deceptively simple, Lu Xun's brief tale provokes thought about a particular cultural and political situation in China, but also on a universal human moment. It is in the midst of huge shifts in human affairs that light is shed, in odd moments, on our own particular condition, and a tiny incident shifts our perception of ourselves and of the larger world. We are taken out of our lazy and disconnected selves and questions are presented to us, but no simple answers are provided. And it is the questions themselves that move us forward. A minor incident prompts something of major proportions in our individual lives.

Lu Xun both is and is not the narrator of "A Minor Incident." Even in translation his authorial control is perfect. In a slightly later story entitled "Upstairs in the Tavern" (1924),[23] Lu Xun again employs a first person narrative. The narrator is a traveler from the north to a town in south-east China where he had grown up, and this is a story about memory and the past as it invades the present. This narrator meets an old friend from years back upstairs in the tavern, who proceeds to tell him of two small incidents in his life. The first is the reburying of the man's (he is called Lü Weifu) dead brother's coffin which is being threatened by river floods. The body and coffin in the grave have, in fact, entirely perished, and he reburies only some mud in a new coffin. But then everything that Lü Weifu does is "utterly pointless." The second incident is his attempt to bring some red velvet flowers for the daughter of an old neighbor, a girl called Ah-shun. But the girl dies before he can give her the flowers. He gives them instead to her younger sister, Ah-zhao:

> But what was I to do with those two velvet flowers? I asked her [Ah-shun's mother] to pass them on to Ah-zhao. Not with a particularly good will: Ah-zhao had fled the moment she'd set eyes on me—as if I were a wolf, come to eat her up.... But anyway. Now, all I had to do was tell Mother how pleased Ah-shun had been,

---

23. Lu Xun, *Real Story*, 178–87.

and the job was done. Completely pointless, but the time passes, at least.²⁴

Lü Weifu finally goes back to his life teaching Confucius, commenting, "what a waste of time it all is."

Lu Xun recesses his story behind two "voices"—that of the first person narrator and then the speech of Lü Weifu himself, so that the reader sees this world through a double lens, the past and the present oddly conflated. To my Western eyes part of the oddity of the story emerges out of the use of metaphors that seem strange and slightly stilted in the English translation. For example: "she had a very ordinary sort of face, long and thin like a melon seed, and sallow."²⁵ But the power lies in the detail, and in the context of the tavern and the shifts of temporal distance, the enormous weariness and sense of fruitlessness that is conveyed, the sharpness residing in the elusiveness and the half spoken truths. Once again, there is here a final lack of closure and a questioning at the heart of a culture and society in the process of change and dislocation from its roots both geographically and spiritually.

To read Lu Xun's essays and stories in a modern English translation is an experience within which one quickly becomes aware of their social and cultural remoteness from a reader like myself. Any such writing that is so recessed and evasive through its use of irony and satire, its language games, its allusions and its employment of the subtle devices of rhetoric and narration, is inevitably going to feel strange and slightly unworldly. But oddly, and as such, it also thus becomes part of world literature alongside the writings of Dante, Shakespeare, Goethe and Dostoevsky. Like many great writers, Lu Xun has suffered by becoming the stuff of Chinese education, the "Lu Xun spirit" flattened and packaged in the school text books of mandated study since the 1940s. But equally, like all great writers, his is a spirit that still shines through such educational battering, often enigmatically and sometimes when it is rediscovered in strange new places—such as in the reading of a Western academic like myself with only the most modest sense of Chinese literature and culture, both ancient and modern. In "The Epitaph," Lu Xun, as a speaking corpse, remarks, "When I have turned into dust you will see my smile!"²⁶ The spirit of his literature will live on.

24. Lu Xun, *Real Story*, 187.
25. Lu Xun, *Real Story*, 183.
26. Lu Xun, quoted in Davies, *Lu Xun's Revolution*, 334.

Lu Xun's spirit in his writings is both entirely of his age and yet, like any great literature, it is also of all time. In his essay "Confucius in Modern China" (1935), he writes of the mass of ordinary people in China today, and "especially the so-called 'ignorant commoners,' [who] may call Confucius a sage, but they do not believe he is a sage. They show respect for him, but do not feel close to him."[27] But, he concludes, if the masses are ignorant, "they aren't ignorant to that extent." He suggests that his reader tries to go "barefoot and in rags" into a Confucian temple, into an upmarket Shanghai cinema, or into a first class carriage on the train. He or she will quickly come to realize their place—will quickly "know."

This is typically Lu Xun—prickly, never quite square on, clear yet suggestive, wry and deconstructive, leaving everyone slightly uncomfortable, and just a little wiser in ways that have to be thought about carefully though they are simple at their heart. This fits, perhaps, Michel Foucault's definition of "spirituality" as "researches, practices and experiences, which may be purifications, ascetic exercises, renunciations, conversions of looking, modifications of existence, etc." pursued "not for knowledge" as such but "for the subject's very being, the price to be paid for access to the truth."[28]

In Lu Xun's writing all this becomes, in a way, spiritual medicine for the soul. It may be, after all, that he is a religious writer.

---

27. Lu Xun, *Jottings*, 188.

28. Foucault, *Hermeneutics of the Subject*, 15. See also Davies, *Lu Xun's Revolution*, 232.

10

Response to the Reading of Lu Xun

Ou Guang-an

David's paper on Lu Xun captures the three foremost significant aspects of the writing of this literary giant in modern China, namely spirit as a saving force for an "apathetically" devastated country, the peculiarity of Lu Xun's language or voice which is, in David's words, "biting, ambiguous, demanding and humane," and the writer's possible status and the feasibility of his entering into the realm of world literature.

Lu Xun's determined action of turning to literature or writing, an "outcry" (appearing mostly in Western translations) for gathering power in the preservation of an ancient nation or even a "call to arms" (in one of the most authoritative translations in China which has been reprinted many times over half a century) as the means to save modern Chinese people and ultimately to save modern China from sinking into an ever more depressed and desolate situation, seems paradoxically to be in contrast to a tradition in ancient China to give up one's literary career in order to enlist in the army to defend the country, with Ban Chao being the most typical example. Since the Spring and Autumn and Warring States period (771–464 BCE) when the major sustaining factors dominating Chinese people's thinking were established to a large extent and remaining up to the time of Lu Xun, a period of almost twenty-five centuries, the main management or governing of China was done according to principles of Confucianism (often mixed with Taoism and Buddhism). The essential governing body of the people consisted almost exclusively of officials, that is, of men of letters (文官) who had to pass a quite complicated system of examinations on subjects chosen from such Confucian literature as *The Great Four Books*

Response to the Reading of Lu Xun | Guang-an

and *The Five Classics*. In other words, over two thousand years of Chinese history before Lu Xun's time though it is the military officials who probably are trained in the martial arts and the arts of war (武 将) that establish a new dynasty or destroy an old one, the real management of culture and society lay in those men of letters who were also supposed to "manage" the thinking or the "spirit" of common Chinese folks with such knowledge as is proposed in works such as the *Analects* or *The Great Learning*. But when we come to the time of Lu Xun, such a form of government encounters a huge barrier and modern China after the Opium Wars with the British (1849–1852 and 1856–1860) went through a "changing situation unprecedented in over three thousand years."[1] This is a quotation from Li Hongzhang, a high-ranking officer who began his career by taking the national examinations but gained his promotion to something like the position of Prime Minister by fighting wars, or in the words of some Western scholars, "China was going through a period of being forced to respond to the first impact from Western powers."[2] For Lu Xun, the incident of his apathetic fellows in the slide show when he was studying medicine in Japan is the moment when he felt the uselessness of saving his fellow countrymen's bodies without saving their "spirit," and more importantly it is the very moment that he felt the helplessness and hopelessness of traditional Chinese culture (Confucianism included). It is then that he would utter the "outcry" regarding the Chinese "spirit"—that which was supposed to have sustained China for over two thousand years, and thus engendering the necessity of new life, the *vita nova*.

Putting Lu Xun in the tradition of Lin Shu and taking the issue of "spirituality" in Lu Xun's writing into the realm of world literature reveal David's acute sensitivity in grasping the idea of "spirit-saving." This is perhaps the haunting theme of Lu Xun's whole life, put into practice by the writer immediately after that incident which so fiercely exposed and criticized the negative sides (the so-called "rooted negativeness") of his fellow Chinese. This still holds its lasting critical power in the eyes of some prestigious scholars on Lun Xun in contemporary China, a time which, as far as these scholars are concerned, is similarly disconcerting and at times disorienting as it was in Lu Xun's day. An interesting thing appears when we discuss the very word "spirit" (let us first put it this way) in Lu Xun's writing. The word used by him in Chinese is 精 神, which is employed usually

1. Liang Qichao, *Biography of Li Hongzhang*, 55.
2. Young-tsu Wong, *Biographical Studies*, 125.

to refer to the kind of being which is the opposite to one's physical body. The Chinese phrase (it has two characters) is normally shortened into one character as 神, as the opposite to another single Chinese character 形. In translation, 形 can be easily rendered as "form or physical form" whereas 神 is more complicated. In the Chinese context, it can sometimes refer to deities in Taoism or folk culture as in 天 神 (literally "heaven gods"), but more often it is used in its two character form as in 精 神, which, in Lu Xun's case, refers to one's "metaphysical" idea or concept or thinking that is opposite to the body but which also controls the body. In either sense Lu Xun's phrase 精 神 is better translated as "spirit," and this is the case for almost all the translations of Lu Xun's works. However, a reader who is familiar with the Western tradition would readily sense also the connotation of "soul" when reading Lu Xun's explanation about his turning to literary writing and reading his writing as a whole. One should remember that Lu Xun began to have contact with Western language and culture in his secondary education and the fact that he studied in a college in Japan, translating several works in foreign languages (Russian and English included). But the idea of "soul" is also intriguing because its usual Chinese translation is 灵 魂, which in turn, in the Chinese context, is composed of two concepts: one is "spirit" 灵 and the other is 魂 which is probably closer to the idea of the English word "soul." Perhaps something similar is to be found in Ernest Hemingway's sentence "a man can be destroyed but not defeated" in his parable-novella *The Old Man and the Sea* (1952) where Hemingway seems to be talking about an idea very close to what Lu Xun means by saying that he is writing to save his fellow countrymen's "spirit." Nevertheless, it is this very complicated sense of "being embedded in Chinese culture" and at the same time the power of Western influence on Lu Xun, obtained as early as his teenage education, that constitute his outcry for the salvation of his fellow countrymen.

It is also this complication that makes Lu Xun's language and his very intention of writing ambivalent, as David observes: "Lu Xun is a writer who speaks most loudly when he fails to speak." Is the exposure of the weakness of his fellow citizens the real intention of his writing? Besides exposing them are there any other possibilities that can save China and Chinese people? Does Ah-Q really know the meaning of *Geming* when he stammers the phrase like a gun machine? Are all his fellow citizens apathetic, poor or depressed people like Ah-Q or those who watched their fellow citizen's head be cut off simply lacking in any sympathy? About all these questions, as David puts it, "we know but do not know, and yet we are provoked into thought." On the one hand, Lu Xun's criticizing of the negative sides of traditional Chinese culture and of his fellow citizens (as shown, for example, in his famous essay "A Madman's Diary") looks towards the revolutionary context which shaped the image of Lu Xun as a sage in the revolution after his death. On the other hand, in a more contemporary context there seems to be an increasing outcry from the reading public for cutting out or reducing the number of Lu Xun's articles (short stories, essays) in textbooks for students, especially in primary and secondary schools, because there is too much darkness and negativity in them. It is now said that when a child of seven or eight years old reads them it is too heavy a burden for them. However, in the meantime there are always some voices from the academic or research fields that call for a proper and appropriate understanding of Lu Xun and his works, and this might be seen as a reflection of the fact that we readers should also investigate that which Lu Xun does "not say" in writing his words. Here Lu Xun can be spoken of as inheriting a tradition of "finite words and infinite meanings" in Chinese writing, that is, in traditional Chinese writing and poetry one is supposed to use a fixed or certain amount of words without actually expressing clearly their intention or meaning. The reader has to decipher the code of the words, while if the writer openly expresses his intention or the meaning then the writing may be considered as poor. Therefore, in Lu Xun's writing, we can certainly understand what Ah-Q means by saying "Geming, Geming, Geming" on one hand, but we also seem to be at a loss to know what Lu Xun precisely means by that. It is certainly a deeply Chinese tradition of writing in which Lu Xun is embedded.

Then, how can Lu Xun be enlisted into the gallery of world literature if he, it seems, is only inheriting Chinese traditions of writing? Professor Jasper precisely notices the fact that Lu Xun's time is a period when "culture and society [is] in the process of change and dislocation from its roots both geographically and spiritually," and Lu Xun's spirit in his writings is "both of his age and yet, like any great literature, of all time." As any Chinese farmer at the beginning of twentieth-century China, we can all be Ah-Q in his self-deception when facing helplessness and, at the same time, yearning for revolution. As a reasonably educated person living in 1920s Peking we can all be that man who sits in the rickshaw scolding the rickshaw runner's making a fuss of a small incident in traffic while still engaging in self-criticism by asking a series of questions after the accident. These moments might be described as universal human moments, when "a tiny incident shifts our perception of ourselves and of the larger world." This meticulously pertinent investigation of one of Lu Xun's seldom-criticized short stories by Professor Jasper is important enough to be in the list of earlier literary critics on Lu Xun, both Western and Chinese, with such names as Harriet Mills, Vera Schwarcz, Xia Ji'an and Li Oufan. There is no escape in an age of change and dislocation, especially for someone like Lu Xun who feels the tremendous responsibility of saving his fellow citizens and ultimately the country itself. In his early life Lu Xun received a strictly traditional education and he is quite proficient in using classic Chinese language to write a scholarly work, his *Short History of Chinese Novels* (1923). It is also interesting to note that his two co-authored translation works are written in classic Chinese. But at another point, he openly suggests to young readers that they should read less, or even no Chinese books but read more "foreign books." With an established Chinese tradition as his background, Lu Xun is seeking at the same time for a way out and when he does do that the scope of his writing (though not the scene or the action) expands far beyond his hometown, his capital city and his country. In the courses and disciplines of Western subjects in middle school, in his studying Western medicine in Japan and in his translating stories of foreign languages (mainly English and Russian), there must have been numerous moments when he had to deal with the comparison or contrast of concepts in modern China and that far beyond modern China. With this reflection in mind as we read and study Lu Xun we may imitate and modify the last sentence in Ah-Q's "true story": we have not followed him entirely in vain.

11

Seeking Christian Theology in Modern Chinese Fiction[1]

An Exercise for Sino-Christian Theology

DAVID JASPER

THIS CHAPTER HAS ITS origins in many and various places. Its theological claims may seem to be extravagant. But as the intelligent project of Christian theology seems to be faltering, perhaps terminally, in Western thought and imagination, then the challenge, as we have seen, is being taken up in its own way in the more recent churches and universities of South Eastern Asia, and in the People's Republic of China in particular. The cultural and intellectual difficulties of a truly Sino-Christian theology extend far beyond the political and social limitations placed upon Christian thought and practice in China, for the difficulty of re-envisioning Christian theology, rooted as it is in the Bible and the categories of Greek philosophy, in the Confucian traditions of Chinese culture may be well-nigh insurmountable. This problem is illustrated in the very title of one important book on Sino-Christian theology, Pan-chiu Lai and Jason Lam's *Sino-Christian Theology: A Theological Qua Cultural Movement in Contemporary China* (2010), which asks the question as to whether we are concerned here with a theological or a cultural matter? Thus, for example, a review of Christian

1. An earlier version of this chapter was published as "Finding Theology in Contemporary Chinese Fiction," *International Journal for the Study of the Christian Church* 19.2–3 (2019) 160–74.

attention to the issue of Christology by Chinese theologians over the last hundred years or so, will reveal that, almost inevitably it seems, Christ emerges as a sage, a social reformer, lacking the dimension of transcendence that Greek philosophy readily supplies.[2] An example of this can be readily found, as we have seen, in the writings of Wu Leichuan (1970–1944) and his influential book *Christianity and Chinese Culture* (1936), guided by proponents of the Social Gospel in Britain and the USA, which emphasizes religion as a force in social progress.[3] In the words of John Y. H. Yieh:

> To show the traditionalists that Christianity did not conflict with Chinese culture, Wu Leichuan introduced Jesus as "*Sheng tianzi*" (holy son of heaven), the sage-king who performed the functions of king, prophet and priest. He also compared the Holy Spirit to the idea of *ren* (benevolence), the highest virtue in Confucianism.[4]

Within the categories of the Confucian culture that continues to characterize contemporary China, Christian theology inevitably tends to become a program for social reform, rooted in the Nestorianism that has theologically always haunted Christianity in China. But this, I wish to argue, is not the end of the story.

The broad study of literature and theology has recently benefited enormously from the work of William Franke and his book *A Theology of Literature* (2017). This is one of those small books that have considerable impact. Beginning with the literature of the Bible, Franke argues for literature as providing that light of revelation that engenders a theology from within the literary traditions of human culture. As Franke puts it, the "ongoing interpretation of human experience is played out in exemplary fashion from the very beginning of the Bible."[5] I want now to develop this theological insight within the further and perhaps unlikely context of some recent Chinese novels. To do this, I enlist also the work of Zhang Longxi, a professor of comparative literature and translation at the City University of Hong Kong, whose recent work seeks to expand the hitherto somewhat Eurocentric concept of "world literature" to embrace the rapidly developing literary tradition of China and South Eastern Asia in expanding

---

2. See above, 93–97, and further, Jasper, "Reflections on the Maturity of Religion," 134.
3. See further Starr, *Chinese Theology*, 128–53.
4. Yieh, "Reading the Sermon on the Mount in China," 146.
5. Franke, *Theology of Literature*, 13.

conversations of cross-cultural understanding.⁶ Finally, I will echo and adapt Maurice Blanchot's idea of *l'espace littéraire*—the space of literature. Within this space, and giving primacy to the literary moment, Blanchot has written of the great Czech writer Franz Kafka, comparing him to the German poet Friedrich Hölderlin: "Kafka's passion is just as purely literary, but it is not always only literary. Salvation is an enormous preoccupation with him, all the stronger because it is hopeless, and all the more hopeless because it is totally uncompromising."⁷ But it is in the space of literature that this passion is engendered—a space that has no theological pretensions within itself, but yet demands a response from theology. It is a field in which the problems and anxieties of theology begin to be articulated or to be re-articulated. It is not the task of literature to articulate or construct any Christian theology, and the novelist is never simply a theologian by another name. But the novelist may explore anew the suffering, joyful narratives that prompt and demand the task of theology with its own creativities and purposes.

Some of the early impetus behind this thinking was inspired long ago by the "postliberal" theology of George A. Lindbeck in his book *The Nature of Doctrine* (1984) in the light of what Lindbeck called "a quarter century of growing dissatisfaction with the usual ways of thinking about those norms of communal belief and action which are generally spoken of as the doctrines or dogmas of churches."⁸ For Lindbeck and his "cultural-linguistic" approach to theology, the task is "intratextual" rather than "extratextual"— the matter of meaning, and this includes religious meaning, lying immanent within the text, constituted by "the uses of a specific language" in the writing.⁹ For literary critics in the early 1980s this would have come as no surprise after the projects of New Criticism and Structuralism,¹⁰ but Christian theology has never been as sensitive as literary criticism to cultural shifts in text and language, and hence we must recognize the particular importance of Lindbeck's book. Other, and perhaps more remote theological roots to this chapter include, perhaps oddly, Thomas J. J. Altizer's radical theology and the death of God, precisely because it is discovered most deeply in a poetics and in literary texts from Dante to James Joyce, denying

---

6. Zhang Longxi, *From Comparison to World Literature*.
7. Blanchot, *Space of Literature*, 57.
8. Lindbeck, *Nature of Doctrine*, 7.
9. Lindbeck, *Nature of Doctrine*, 114.
10. See Culler, *Structuralist Poetics*; Lentricchia, *After the New Criticism*.

any theologically generated sense of the presence of God, and celebrating a profoundly apocalyptic vision that emerges also in the tenor of recent Chinese fiction. Although Altizer has no immediate political concerns, his vision of apocalyptic theology is shared also by the liberation theology of Peruvian pastor and theologian Gustavo Gutiérrez, with his references also to Marxist theory and his utopian hope for this world.[11] Finally, I am led by the French thinker Jean-Luc Marion to reflect upon the idea of the "saturated phenomenon" (of which Christ himself is the primary example) as that in which "intuition passes beyond the concept"[12]—a concept that is at once essentially simple and at the same time profoundly ungraspable. This quality I also find, disturbingly, in the modern and contemporary Chinese fiction to which I now turn.

In his celebrated novel *Silence* (1969) the Christian Japanese novelist Shūsaku Endō confronts us with a complex theological mystery found in the silence of God in the context of the seventeenth-century persecutions of Christians in Japan. In modern China Lu Xun (1881–1936), who, as we have seen, set out as a young man, so he tells us, to save the spirit of his people through writing literature, confronts us even further with no God in an ancient Chinese culture that in the early twentieth century was struggling to move from ancient cultural complacencies in the late Qing dynasty into the new world of the Republic that began to emerge after 1911. The Western reader, reading in translation more often than not, quickly discovers that it is extremely hard to find a foothold in Lu Xun's stories. It is partly that their Chinese language, full of puns, odd metaphors and repetitions, is so hard to translate into English, but far more than that, they seem to embrace a world that is entirely self-enclosed, shutting out all other connections and external references.

We might return to the superficially similar conclusions of Lu Xun's novella "The Real Story of Ah-Q" (1921)[13] with the ending of the German writer Patrick Süskind's celebrated novel *Perfume* (1985). Süskind's conclusion plays with macabre, gothic horror on the imagery of the Christian Eucharist—a human body dismembered and utterly consumed by the crowd, ending in the, provocative, shocking final sentence: "For the first

---

11. See Gutiérrez, *Essential Writings*, 184–235.

12. Marion, *Being Given*, 199.

13. Even the title of this novella defies any simple translation, playing with the idea of the real/true story—and somehow edged beyond the notion of "truth."

time they had done something out of Love."[14] "Ah-Q" also ends with the execution of the central character. These are final words of the story:

> Public opinion in Weizhuang was undivided: of course Ah-Q was a villain—he wouldn't have been shot otherwise. The verdict in town was more ambivalent: death by a firing-squad, the majority of them felt, wasn't a patch on decapitation. And the condemned had been a miserable specimen. In that whole extended tour around the streets, he hadn't managed to choke out a single line of opera; they had followed him for nothing.[15]

"Public opinion," then, can hide behind the final decision of the authority of the state: Ah-Q is found guilty, and within the protection of that assurance, manifold, amoral and utterly self-centered positions are available. Ah-Q, in short, is fair game. Even Lu Xun's slippery narrator partakes of all such relativities, as his translator Julia Lovell has remarked: "our condescending narrator, we realize, is a thoroughly compromised man who slips between the various worlds he parodies."[16] And finally Lu Xun himself refused to be pinned down as regards his story, commenting that "I wrote *The Real Story* with the intention of exposing the weakness of my fellow citizens—I did not specify whether or not I myself was included therein."[17]

At the same time this troubling narrative opens up a space, a space of literature, that is immune from all controlling spheres of power, be they political or theological. This space might, however, be illumined by the definition of "spirituality" as offered by Michel Foucault,[18] whose last lectures, we should recall, explored exercises of power and the place of "truth acts"—that is, the place of individuals within procedures of truth-telling in relation to power and its absolutization. (In some of his final words Foucault explores such "truth acts" in early Christian writings and practices of spiritual direction.)[19] Foucault's claim that "there can be no truth without a conversion or a transformation of the subject"[20] has been applied by Gloria Davies to the spaces of Lu Xun's fictions, their exposures and their

---

14. Süskind, *Perfume*, 263
15. Lu Xun, *Real Story of Ah-Q*, 123.
16. Lovell, "Introduction," xxiii.
17. Liu, *Translingual Practice*, 70.
18. See also above 117.
19. See Foucault, *On Government*.
20. Foucault, quoted in Davies, *Lu Xun's Revolution*, 232.

possibilities. These have been explored in some detail in the earlier chapter on the writings of Lu Xun.

While he was still a student in Tokyo in 1907, Lu Xun together with his brother Zhou Zuoren and some other Chinese students, founded a new journal of which the purpose was the revival of the classics of Chinese literature. Its title, "which was derived from the idea of creating 'new life,'"[21] was *Vita Nova*, but it failed even before its first edition was produced and only forty-one copies were sold. Nevertheless it served to emphasize the continuing link between modern Chinese literature and the Chinese Classics, to which I will return later. Such literary connections are certainly apparent in the novels of Yu Hua (1960–), examples of what has become known as "scar literature" written in the aftermath of the period of Mao Zedong and the Cultural Revolution of 1966–1976. Born in the eastern coastal province of Zhejiang, Yu Hua attended high school during the Cultural Revolution and was a dentist before turning to literature in 1983. He has since won international acclaim winning, among other prizes, the James Joyce Foundation Award. The comparison with the early career of Lu Xun is notable. Yu Hua's best-known work, the novel *To Live* (1993), seems clearly to be written within the ancient Daoist tradition of submissiveness to fate and the inevitable upon which Guang-an has written at length in his reading of Thomas Hardy's *Tess of the D'Urbervilles*.[22] The precise nature of the central term of this tradition, *wu wei*, is extremely difficult to capture in English, but it is a key term in the writings of Chuang Tzu who is perhaps the most spiritual of the classic Chinese philosophers. Literally it means "doing nothing" but it is actually more positive than that, suggesting more "not doing anything against the flow."[23] The Trappist monk Thomas Merton was moved to write an extended meditation on the Daoist tradition in his book *The Way of Chuang Tzu* (1965) in which he is quite clear that his work is the very opposite of any attempt to "find" Christianity in the Chinese tradition:

> This book is not intended to prove anything or to convince anyone of anything that he does not want to hear about in the first place. In other words, it is not a new apologetic subtlety . . . in which

---

21. Preface to *Outcry* in Lu Xun, *Jottings*, 21. *Outcry* was the title of Lu Xun's first collection of short stories, published in 1923.

22. See above, 34–55.

23. Chuang Tzu, *Inner Chapters*, xiv–xvii.

Christian rabbits will suddenly appear by magic out of a Taoist hat.[24]

And in the same comparative spirit, I return to Yu Hua's *To Live*. An extraordinary Chinese film of this novel, in which Yu Hua was involved, was initially banned in the People's Republic of China, though it was widely available in the West. *To Live* follows the life of Fugui in first person narrative from a carefree and prosperous youth to an impoverished, patient old age. It is framed within an introduction and conclusion by the young "author" who encounters Fugui in the country when he "had the carefree job of going into the countryside to collect popular folk songs."[25]

The final scene in the book, like the first, sees Fugui ploughing with his old ox, an image of utter resignation—or perhaps something like *wu wei*:

> *The old man and his ox gradually got farther away, but from far off I could still hear the echo of the old man's hoarse and moving voice. It floated through the open night like the wind. The old man sang:*
>
> In my younger days I wandered amuck,
> At middle age I wanted to stash everything in a trunk,
> And now that I'm old I've become a monk.[26]

Yu Hua himself has expressed most precisely the heart of his fictional character:

> After going through much pain and hardship, Fugui is inextricably tied to the experience of suffering. So there is really no place for ideas like "resistance" in Fugui's mind—he lives simply to live. In this world I have never met anyone who has as much respect for life as Fugui.[27]

Yu Hua writes within the literary tradition of Lu Xun. As we have seen both writers began their careers within the field of medicine, in Yu Hua's case as a dentist. The uncompromising violence of his novels elicited the remark from his fellow writer Mo Yan: "I've heard that [Yu Hua] was a dentist for five years. I can't imagine what kind of brutal tortures patients endured

---

24. Merton, *Way of Chuang Tzu*, 10.
25. Yu Hua, *To Live*, 3.
26. Yu Hua, *To Live*, 235.
27. Yu Hua, *To Live*, 244.

under his cruel steel pliers."[28] But perhaps pain is sometimes necessary in the process of cure and healing.

Even in their English translations one senses the linguistic experimentation and the radical, often painful, dissection of the soul of the Chinese people in Yu Hua's novels like *To Live* or *Chronicle of a Blood Merchant* (1996), each a novel of its time and place and yet disturbingly mythic and universal. In *Chronicle of a Blood Merchant*, the central character, Xu Sanguan, supplements his meager income to support his family by frequent visits to the local blood chief. But donating his blood for his family, he discovers that his wife has been unfaithful—but in the end ties of kin prove stronger than anything. In the words of the novel's English translator, Andrew F. Jones, referring to Xu Sanguan and his son (who is not his son) Yile: "And what ultimately counts most for Yile and his father is not so much blood but a simple term of address, a signal that cuts through the noise, an inaccurate yet redemptive fiction: 'Dad.'"[29] Yu Hua's novels are immersed in a culture with philosophical, socio-cultural, and religious roots that are deeply Chinese, and also a more recent history that is still remote and almost unknown to most Western readers. Nevertheless they speak with a powerful, urgent and universal voice that opens up spaces for questions that resonate within all religious traditions and prompt humane conversations across the barriers of faith, history and culture.

The world of the fiction of the novelist Yan Lianke is far from that of Yu Hua. Born in Henan Province, Yan Lianke began his work as a writer for the army. Initially a member of the Communist Party, a number of Yan Lianke's novels were banned and he was forced to write self-criticisms. His satirical novel *Serve the People!* (2005) is set in the year 1967, the second of Mao Zedong's Cultural Revolution. Although the author is now Professor of Creative Writing at Renmin University of China in Beijing at the very heart of the Chinese political and cultural establishment, the novel, like its successor *Dream of Ding Village* (2006) on the blood contamination in Henan Province, remains banned by the Chinese government. The *South China Post* quoted the words of the propaganda department: "This novella slanders Mao Zedong, the army, and is overflowing with sex. Do not distribute, pass around, comment on, excerpt from or report on it." Such is the paradox of China and the vitality of literature as the novel found wide underground readership. *Serve the People!* is written very much in the style of

---

28. Mo Yan, quoted in Yu Hua, *To Live*, 239.
29. Jones, "Afterword," 263.

the Czech writer Jaroslav Hašek's *The Good Soldier Švejk and His Fortunes in the World War* (1921) and begs comparison with the foundational literature of Rabelais in its deliberate and satirical excesses. But Yan Lianke, of relatively humble birth in rural China, speaks for those who have no voice, who are forgotten and trampled upon. Of his own writing he has suggested:

> Passion and anger are the driving force of my novels. Writers should pay attention to the emotional lives of the masses, births, deaths, and intolerable humiliation, the desperate situations of their existences. They are the majority but our literature happens to have abandoned them.[30]

The relentless, satirical tone of *Serve the People!* allows the reader little resting place, the narrative endlessly disorientating, discomforting and disrupting while at the same time funny. The central character, the soldier Wu Dawang, is a humble sergeant of the Catering Squad, who is seduced by his military commander's young wife, Liu Lian, prompting an illicit erotic game between the two of them that involves smashing or destroying the "sacred" symbols of the Revolution—statues of Mao, copies of the *Little Red Book*, epigrams of the Great Helmsman.

Yan Lianke sets out to be deliberately iconoclastic. Yet, oddly, the radical nature of the narrative provokes, in a way like Lu Xun, literary reminiscences of the great narrative parables of St Luke's Gospel with their stretched language, their surrealism and their refusal to allow conclusion, uncomfortably provoking thought. In its exposure of the corruption and insanity of the Cultural Revolution one might almost say of Yan Lianke's novel what Sallie McFague once wrote of the parable of the Prodigal Son:

> One *could* paraphrase this parable in the theological assertion "God's love knows no bounds," but to do that would be to miss what the parable can do for our insight into such love. For what *counts* here is not extricating an abstract concept but precisely the opposite, delving into the details of the story itself, letting the metaphor do its job of revealing the new setting for ordinary life. It is the play of the radical images that does the job.[31]

Serve the People! is uncomfortable and unsettling even while it is being very funny, a narrative always refusing assertion and abstraction. Yan Lianke opens the book with a comment on the nature of the novel as a genre:

---

30. Yan Lianke, *Serve the People!*.
31. McFague, *Speaking in Parables*, 15.

> The novel is the only place for a great many of life's truths. Because it is only in fiction that certain facts can be held up to light.
> The novel it is, then, for this particular truth.
> The story I'm about to tell you, you see, bears some resemblance to real characters and events.
> Or, if I may put it this way: life has imitated art.[32]

In the liveliness of the fiction we move beyond all definitions of theology, doctrine or dogma, whether religious or political, its disruptions always a provocation to further thought and reflection upon truth.

It was in a seminar held in Renmin University of China in Beijing that I first met Yan Lianke. Present at the seminar also was a woman novelist who is still in the early years of her career as a writer—Sheng Keyi, though now she writes in North America. Her most recent novel, *Death Fugue* (2014), has apocalyptic overtones as well as deliberate echoes of Paul Celan, but it is her first novel, *Northern Girls: Life Goes On* (2004) with which I am concerned here. Like Yu Hua, Sheng Keyi is rooted in traditional Chinese culture and, it might be said, its spirituality, though her concerns are relentlessly contemporary and drawing on her own experience as a Chinese woman. *Northern Girls* follows the life of Qian Xiaohong, a young girl from rural Hunan province, as she struggles to make her way in the world of the modern Chinese city. In her "Afterword" to the novel, Sheng Keyi writes:

> Qian Xiaohong is a familiar figure to me. She is typical of the people from my home village. When I started her story, I planned simply to write about the village, but once I began, I felt the place to be too restrictive for such a character. I wanted to toss her out into the wider world and see what she was destined to experience. Through the eyes of Qian Xiaohong and her companions—as well as the testimony of their bodies—we feel the cruel realities of the times and the difficulty of surviving.[33]

Sheng Keyi's concerns are determinedly issues in contemporary China with its fast pace of development: urbanization, social dislocation, gender and the place of women in what is still a profoundly patriarchal and essentially traditional society. But to readers who are familiar with the Bible, her narratives once again sound familiar echoes (though perhaps unknown to the author herself)—in *Northern Girls* of the parable of the Prodigal Son, though here there is no return and no forgiveness for Qian Xiaohong, some

32. Yan Lianke, *Serve the People!*, 1.
33. Sheng Keyi, *Northern Girls*, 319.

of the women in the gospels, and the decay of society as addressed in the prophetic tradition of the Hebrew Bible. And also, as with the character of Fugui in *To Live*, but without his song and through gritted teeth, there is something of that ancient Daoist quality of resignation, but there is now a deeper note of fatalism. Yet still Qian Xiaohong does survive despite her marginalization in Chinese society. The novel ends with the girl vanishing into the life of the city, becoming one with it:

> Gritting her teeth, she bent her head and . . . she stood. She trudged out of the ring of feet surrounding her and pushed her way down from the pedestrian bridge.
> Then she faded into the crowds on the street.[34]

We have heard, then, a few fictional voices from the China of the tumultuous twentieth century and now the twenty-first century also. In these novels they are not the voices of the great and the powerful but almost always of people from the bottom rungs of modern Chinese society. Beginning with the unstable, satirical narratives of Lu Xun all of them echo something of the spirituality of ancient China that has never quite been crushed by the communist revolution, preserved, almost unconsciously at times, in the urge for self-expression found in writers and novelists who are only now beginning to be read and heard in the self-obsessed countries of Europe and North America. Even though he won the Nobel Prize for literature in 2000, by which time he was writing in exile in France, the novelist Gao Xingjian is still little read in the West. His great novel *Soul Mountain* (*Lingshan*) (1990, first published in Taiwan) searches, like Lu Xun before had done, the "soul" of the Chinese people in a nonconformity that reaches deep into the literature and spirituality of what Karl Jaspers has dubbed the Axial Age of ancient wisdom in the almost contemporary Chinese Classics and the Hebrew Bible. Only now, in the work of scholars of comparative literature like Zhang Longxi are we beginning to explore a poetics of world literature, at the heart of which lie profound and ultimately universal religious questions[35] concerning creation and creativity.

Yet if modern Chinese literature is still barely on the curriculum of comparative literary studies in the colleges and universities of the west, the literature that I have been reviewing carries disturbing echoes that sound from a non-Christian context, of the preoccupations of Christian liberation

---

34. Sheng Keyi, *Northern Girls*, 318.
35. See Jasper, Review, 121–23.

theology as it has welled up from South America in the writings of Gustavo Gutiérrez and others. In situations of oppression and the silencing of the majority they share a sense of the need to embrace the complexity of the world and avoid in both theology and literature equally the dangerous simplifications of populism, not least religious populism.[36] Oddly they share a sense of what Gutiérrez, as a Christian priest, finds in prayer, that is a need in human life ground down by utilitarian necessity for time that is "wasted," a free time to celebrate simply the gratuitousness of created being, though sometimes even this must be through gritted teeth.[37] Then writers like Sheng Keyi, Yan Lianke and Yu Hua share with Christian liberation theologians (with whom they might seem to have so little in common) a sense of the nature of that poverty in society that may be profoundly material but which is eventually something much more than that. As Gutiérrez expresses it:

> Social classes, nations and entire continents are becoming aware of their poverty, and when they see its root causes, they rebel against it. We are facing a collective poverty which creates bonds of solidarity among those who suffer it and leads them to organize to struggle against this situation and against those who benefit from it.[38]

Writers like Gao Xingjian and Yan Lianke, who are still silenced in the People's Republic of China, write yet in expressions of the spirit that lives despite repression and coercion. Their literature offers hope and a space for a creative theology—and with that we begin to return to where we began our discussion in this chapter, in the "cultural-linguistic alternative" of George Lindbeck's *Nature of Doctrine*. Lindbeck's description of this in his examination of religion and experience is, in his own term, "pretheological."[39] This is explored in terms of story and narrative—the materials of the novelist's craft. In Lindbeck's words:

> A comprehensive scheme or story used to structure all dimensions of existence is not primarily a set of propositions to be believed, but is rather *the medium in which one moves, a set of skills that one employs in living one's life.* Its vocabulary of symbols and its syntax may be used for many purposes, only one of which is the

---

36. Gutiérrez, *Essential Writings*, 107.
37. Gutiérrez, *Essential Writings*, 289.
38. Gutiérrez, *Essential Writings*, 293.
39. Lindbeck, "Religion and Experience," 30–45.

formulation of statements about reality. Thus while a religion's truth claims are often of the utmost importance to it (as in the case of Christianity), it is, nevertheless, the conceptual vocabulary and the syntax or inner logic which determines the kind of truth claims that religion can make. The cognitive aspect, while often important, is not primary.[40]

It is within this lived medium of experience that we may encounter what the Roman Catholic philosopher and phenomenologist Jean-Luc Marion calls the "saturated phenomenon" within the "given" of being, well described by Robyn Hormer, the English translator of Marion's book *In Excess: Studies of Saturated Phenomena* (2002) in this way: "givenness as the sole horizon of phenomena, and the possibility of phenomena that saturate intuition to such an extent that all horizons are shattered."[41]

Such a possibility describes well the disturbance and sometimes shock that is felt (rather than cognitively constructed), even in translation, in the fiction of Lu Xun, Yan Lianke and the other Chinese writers we have visited, earning some of them the wrath of the political censor, and all of them some claim to be speaking the nation's conscience, recovering its "spirit." Chapter 72 of *Soul Mountain*[42] lays open the nature of the genre of the novel and its "mode of narrative." The writing transforms into a cascade of images and references—a space of literature that links all life with the spiritual:

> In the dispute between form and content and meaningful images and meaningless content about the definition of meaning about everyone wanting to be God about the worship of idols by atheists and self worship being dubbed philosophy about self love about indifference to sex transforming into megalomania about schizophrenia about sitting in Chan contemplation about sitting not in Chan contemplation about meditation about the Way of nurturing the body is not the Way about effability or ineffability but the absolute necessity for the effability of the Way about fashion about revolt against vulgarity is a mighty smash with a racquet about a fatal blow with a club and Buddhist enlightenment[43]

And so it goes on . . .

40. Lindbeck, "Religion and Experience," 35 (emphasis added).

41. Horner, "Translator's Introduction," ix.

42. Guang-an pointed out to me that the number seventy-two immediately links this contemporary Chinese novel with the Chinese classic sixteenth-century "novel" *Journey to the West*. As a Western reader, this resonance and reference eluded me entirely.

43. Gao Xingjian, *Soul Mountain*, 454–56.

In what sense, therefore, and in conclusion, should the pursuit of a Sino-Christian theology be alert to the "secular" literature of contemporary China, rooted, even in its sense of modernity, in the deep cultural roots of Chinese society and its literary history? Is it that, once the profound philosophical (and spiritual) *differences* between Christian theology in western culture, so deeply grounded in the Bible and ancient Greek philosophy, and Chinese culture founded upon ancient Daoism and texts of Confucius, have been acknowledged, then also their profound *connections* should also and equally be recognized.[44] In a remarkable essay entitled "The Contemporary significance of Theological Ethics," Yang Huilin, a distinguished professor of comparative literature at Renmin University of China in Beijing, compares the experiences of Auschwitz and the Cultural Revolution (through which he himself lived). Yang writes:

> In at least two dimensions they link together the experiences of horror and survival in both East and West, which entailed (1) the fantasies and fanaticism of collective unconsciousness, and the uncontrollability of the two combined; and (2) the frailty of humankind's existing values, order, and standards.[45]

Bearing in mind such common experiences, and the capacity, in spite of all differences, for the voice of literature to be heard and felt across all cultural divides in novels which I have here touched upon, and these novels are but a tiny selection taken from a rapidly growing library of contemporary Chinese literature being now translated, we return finally to the project of Sino-Christian theology.

The term, as we have seen, was first used during the 1980s, largely among the so-called "cultural Christians," unbaptized but sympathetic to the Christian faith, who were to be found among the Chinese intellectuals in the universities of the People's Republic of China. Thus, and distinct from other Christian expressions in China today, Sino-Christian theology is primarily an academic exercise addressing the profound philosophical differences between cultures and the task of Christian theology to negotiate them intellectually.[46] But it cannot only be an intellectual enterprise. For as Chloë Starr has emphasized at the beginning of her recent book *Chinese Theology: Text and Context* (2016), "literary form and theological content

---

44. See also Geng Youzhuang, *Between East and West*.
45. Yang Huilin, *China, Christianity*, 61.
46. See, for example, Yang Huilin, "Value of Theology," 101–22.

are indivisible."⁴⁷ Thus as we embark anew and in a new cultural context upon the theological project the Chinese literary forms within which theology finally has its being, need to be acknowledged and experienced. For example, Starr notes how Chinese texts, both ancient and modern, tend to be "relational"—and thus Chinese theology may be also. Starr enlarges upon her observation:

> A common heritage in the Chinese classics and a reading pattern that proceeds via a series of implicit associations in the mind of the reader create a more participative and open-ended way of reading and of engaging with theology. It is a theology that does not just draw from the church and reflect back church thinking, but asks readers to comment on and add to the debates as the texts are written and circulated.⁴⁸

When I first read these words I realized immediately that they illuminated my struggle to read fictional writers like Lu Xun as much as directing me towards a way of engaging with theology. In the elusive, often implicit moves of a fiction that was "saturated" with the phenomenal life of post-1911 China, new and passionate spaces for "doing theology" were opened up, spaces that did not reduce the necessary intellectual challenges but at the same time suggested new ways of thinking and dialogue that offered previously unrecognized opportunities of discussion. Are we perhaps close here to the spiritual vocation that Lu Xun saw as his as a writer for his people in their lassitude in the face of violence and suffering, writing in the "Preface" to his first collection of short stories: "The first task was to change their spirit; and literature and the arts, I decided at the time, were the best means to this end."⁴⁹

Literature, in its task of liberation, and theology, finally, cannot be separated.

---

47. Starr, *Chinese Theology*, 3.
48. Starr, *Chinese Theology*, 3.
49. Lu Xun, quoted in Lovell, "Introduction," xvii.

12

Response to Seeking Christian Theology in Modern Chinese Fiction

Ou Guang-an

As in reading David's chapter on Lu Xun and his novels, and then reading the chapter on modern Chinese fiction, I could not help being moved by David's acute grasping of the essential elements in this fiction, concerning Daoism in particular. But I could not agree more when David points out that though there are profound philosophical differences between Western culture and Chinese culture we should also equally recognize their profound, often literary, connections.

There is no doubt that Daoism and Confucian texts are two of the most important influential factors in Chinese history and culture. And it is also true, as David recognizes, that between these two, Daoism is the school of thought that focuses more on the discussion of spirituality than Confucianism. However, that argument does not exclude the fact that for Confucius and his disciples some discussions of spiritual matters do exist.

In Book VII of *Analects*, there is a famous saying of Confucius: "The subjects on which the Master did not talk, were—extraordinary things, feats of strength, disorder, and spiritual beings."[1] In his footnote to this translation, James Legge, the renowned Sinologist and the first professor of Chinese in the University of Oxford, specifically explains that what Confucius did was not refuse to talk about these subjects at all but rather the

---

1. Confucius, *Confucian Analects* [Legge], 201.

"avoiding" of these subjects in his conversation.[2] Another famous Sinologist, Arthur Waley, almost agrees with Legge in the translation of these subjects but changes the last into a more specific term: "The Master never talked of prodigies, feats of strength, disorders or spirits."[3] Then what are these "spiritual beings" or "spirits" in the Confucian context, or more broadly, in ancient Chinese culture? Two instances in which Confucius does talk about "spirits" probably would suffice to illustrate my point. On one occasion, when one of his intimate disciples asked Confucius about serving the spirits of the dead, the Master answered: "While you are not able to serve men, how can you serve their spirits"?[4] On another occasion: "He sacrificed to the spirits, as if the spirits were present. The Master said, 'I consider my not being present at the sacrifice, as if I did not sacrifice.'"[5] With these two examples, the meaning of "spirit" or "spiritual-being" comes to the surface. That is, to Confucius, on the one hand, a "spirit" is the thing, or the form, or perhaps just the being that is the opposite of the body. On the other hand, the "spirit" is one's "ghost" after one's body has ceased to live, and this, it may be suggested, is the subject that Confucius would rather avoid in his conversation.

The dual feature of "spirit" (in Chinese the character 神), one being the opposite mode of being from a physical body and the other being a "ghost," also pervades the texts of Daoism such as *Zhuangzi*. Further investigation on the question of "spirit" in the Daoist context would reveal that this dual feature is invariably related to the central concept in Daoism— Dao (or Tao). In Book XII of *Zhuangzi*, the writer (Zhuangzi or perhaps his followers) says: "As the Record says, 'Those who are well versed in Tao will accomplish anything; those who have no desires for achievement will subdue the ghosts and spirits.'"[6] In Book XIX of the same work the Duke Huan of Qi was once hunting in the swamps and reported that he saw a "ghost." Upon returning to his palace, he fell ill and did not appear in the court for several days. One of his courtiers, a sage man, it is said, came to the palace and told the duke that he was ill because the breath, or more famously the *qi*, did not go well inside his body.[7] Besides absorbing the idea

---

2. Confucius, *Confucian Analects* [Legge], 201.
3. Confucius, *Analects* [Waley], 87.
4. Confucius, *Confucian Analects* [Legge], 240.
5. Confucius, *Confucian Analects* [Legge], 159.
6. Zhuangzi, *Zhuangzi*, 173, 175.
7. Zhuangzi, *Zhuangzi*, 307, 309.

of "spirit" into the meaning of "ghost," other cases in *Zhuangzi* that discuss the question of "spirit" would take it as the opposite of the "physical body." The spirit can be held together with the physical body and it can also leave one's physical form, which then becomes unimportant. What is important is that the keeping of both one's spirit and one's physical form should conform to the way of Dao. He who wants to be rid of the burden of nourishing his physical form had better abandon all worldly affairs. By abandoning worldly affairs, he will be able to stay away from these things and he will be able to keep a pure and calm heart; by keeping a pure and calm heart, he will be able to interact with nature; by interacting with nature, he will be able to approach Tao.[8]

Both the *Analects* and *Zhuangzi* are classics of a particular period in Chinese history—the period of the Spring and Autumn and Warring States (ca. 770–221 BCE), when different schools of thoughts existed side by side and contended with each other. The dual idea of "spirit" continues to influence the later philosophers in Chinese history, with more emphasis on the opposition between one's physical form and one's "metaphysical" existence. Wang Chong, the famous philosopher who was said to be a follower of Daoism, in the first century CE, argued that when one's body ceases to exist, one's spirit is also gone with it and thus there is no such thing as a ghost. It can be shown that Wang Chong's idea, normally considered as a materialist view, still to some extent accepted the concept of the existence of spirit as opposed to one's body. Major traditions after Confucius's time in Chinese history continued the discussion and the concept of this duality in spirit and body remains so popular that even the general populace would readily recognize it immediately. When we reflect on Confucius's or Zhuangzi's discussion of spirit, it seems that for them it is more of a philosophical question, while later generations would add something more to it, for example, the opposition between the strength in one's physical form and the strength in one's spiritual form. For most of the cases, the spiritual strength occupies the more prominent and significant position. But this is the case, I would argue, both in Western culture and Chinese culture. An immediate example in Western literature is the old fisherman Santiago in *The Old Man and the Sea* (1952).[9] A similar example in Chinese literature would be found in the writings of Lu Xun.

---

8. Zhuangzi, *Zhuangzi*, 297.
9. See also above, 120.

Response to Seeking Theology in Chinese Fiction | Guang-an

When Lu Xun saw the slide show that illustrated how some Chinese men were standing apathetically watching the Japanese soldier about to cut off the head of a fellow Chinese who was charged with being a spy, he was shocked by the fact that these fellow countrymen seemed physically strong but their spirits were broken and helpless. Lu Xun would readily acknowledge that the key to save such a weak country as modern China must be to wake up the peoples' spiritual strength and the right way to achieve that goal is through literature, thus revealing the inseparability of salvation and literature. For most cases, Lu Xun's approach towards salvation by means of literature was to expose the negative sides of Chinese characters, such as Ah-Q in "The Real Story of Ah-Q" or Sister Xianglin in "Blessing." However, what happened in "A Minor Incident" will make us realize that salvation can also be achieved in small incidents in life by such common people as a rickshaw runner. Among contemporary Chinese novelists, David particularly mentions Gao Xinjiang and his representative work, the great novel *Soul Mountain*. In its original title "soul" is 灵 in Chinese characters, and the character 灵 can also be translated as "spirit" in English. Among the works investigated by David in his essay, *Soul Mountain* is the most experimental in terms of writing technique. The most eccentric chapter is chapter 72, in which the author abruptly announces at the very beginning that "this is not a novel." When one reads through the chapter, it comes to an end with quite a long paragraph that has no punctuation at all. David quotes at length from this passage. One would argue that the lack of punctuation is not so surprising because all ancient Chinese novels or works are without punctuation, but one should remember that *Soul Mountain* was written in the 1980s when punctuation had been introduced to China almost one and half centuries before. Whereas anyone who is familiar with English literature would immediately bear in mind that the punctuationless paragraph echoes the last chapter in James Joyce's *magnum opus Ulysses* while the abrupt interruption in the novel's narration to discuss the writing of a novel is reminiscent of Book Second, Chapter XVII (with the title "In which the story pauses a little") of George Eliot's *Adam Bede* (1859). On the other hand, anyone who reads very much about Chinese literature or culture would have no difficulty in guessing, if not recognizing, that the reason that Gao Xinjiang makes the abrupt interruption in chapter 72 is almost certainly because the number seventy-two is the number of changes that the Monkey King could make and transform in *Journey to the West*, one of the four most generally agreed important ancient Chinese classic novels. Is the journey in *Soul Mountain* written in a coincidental intertextuality with the journey in *Journey to the West*? If it is, the number of all the chapters in *Soul Mountain*, as eighty-one, would be much easier to understand, because that is the number of difficulties or hardships that the Monkey King and his master and two brothers have to encounter and overcome. The numbers and the incidents show a remarkable relationship to Buddhism and *Journey to the West* is generally recognized as a work based on Buddhism. And Buddhism, Confucianism and Daoism, are generally considered as the three most important influences on Chinese culture and thought.

Concluding Conversations

13

Concluding Reflections

David Jasper

As we have seen at the conclusion of the last chapter and in Guang-an's response to it, almost at the end of the Nobel Prize winning Gao Xingjian's long picaresque novel *Soul Mountain* (1990, English translation 2000), there is a brief chapter, a kind of excursus, which discusses the nature of fiction and the novel. To an English reader it is reminiscent of George Eliot's similar chapter in *Adam Bede*. It ends with the sentence: "Reading this chapter is optional but as you've read it you've read it."[1] Reading it is, then, hardly an option.

The chapter begins with an outraged exclamation that comes from the direction or voice of the confused reader—you or me: "This isn't a novel!"[2] Indeed—what have we been reading, in my case reading compulsively, for so long? It seems like a literary rag-bag of stories and interludes loosely built around the wanderings of a Beijing writer in the mountainous backwoods of China. The question is asked, can fiction be written "without conforming to the method which is common knowledge?" Or is literature simply non-conformist, deliberately defying our expectations, and how far can it stray from the demands of the generically familiar? In *Soul Mountain* there are not even identifiable characters. Pronouns—I, he, she, you—are employed loosely, almost interchangeably, and without referential clarity as regards personalities, in "petulant exchanges." Finally, the "critic" in this conversation in chapter 72 of this "novel" dismisses this Chinese writer (who is, of

---

1. Gao Xingjian, *Soul Mountain*, 455.
2. Gao Xingjian, *Soul Mountain*, 452.

course, writing all of this) as merely copying Western literature, though without much success: "This is modernist, it's imitating the West but falling short."[3] A sophisticated writer in one culture is simply adopting the contemporary traits of another culture, and so in effect this is just another example of Western cultural imperialism.

"He then says it's Eastern." The author writes of himself in the third person, in the defensive, denying that there are any "models" in the ancient traditions of Chinese writings: from the "gazetteers of the Warring States period" to the "episodic novels and belles-lettres of the Ming and Qing Dynasties" there were never "any fixed models" in literary forms.[4] Of course I am of necessity reading *Soul Mountain* in an English translation (rendered from the Chinese by an Australian academic, Mabel Lee of the University of Sydney). The "author" ("He") resorts to claims for the freedom of literature, asserting simply that "he writes to amuse himself" without any ideological bias. Like a smoke-screen the pronouns take over: "It's just like in the book where *you* is the reflection of *I* and *he* is the back of *you*, the shadow of a shadow. Although there's no face it still counts as a pronoun."[5]

Without a clear conversation partner, the critic departs with some petulance. We are beyond the realm of criticism, literature finally claiming sovereignty. Indeed, the very concept of criticism of fiction is here in question. The last two pages of chapter 72 (this reader wonders, with a degree of helplessness, what they might be like in Chinese) abandon (in English) all rules of grammar and punctuation and resort to a kind of critical or creative stream of consciousness. Where does criticism begin—in literary form, or the self, or action, or language? Or is it a question of politics, or religion (at last), which is mixed up with self ("everyone wanting to be God"[6]) and so inevitably religious reflections begin on "the Way" (*Dao*) and Buddhism, and then on to racism and finally, inevitably perhaps, revolution and the place of literature in the contemporary Chinese People's Republic: "If one has to fall about revolutionary fiction which smashes superstitious belief in literature about a revolution in fiction about revolutionizing fiction."[7]

The reading of these breathless words, an optional exercise only after one has necessarily read them, is a reminder of why the *freedom* of literature

---

3. Gao Xingjian, *Soul Mountain*, 453.
4. Gao Xingjian, *Soul Mountain*, 453.
5. Gao Xingjian, *Soul Mountain*, 454 (emphasis added).
6. Gao Xingjian, *Soul Mountain*, 454.
7. Gao Xingjian, *Soul Mountain*, 455.

matters so much. Freedom is, after all, of its very essence. Between the literature of China and the literature of the West there is clearly, inevitably, an affinity, yet there are also profound differences that defy translation. Our readings and conversations in this present book confirm this truth in literature. It is literature that enables such conversations to take place, but immediately they are confounded by the stumbling blocks and barriers of language, religion, cultural and philosophical differences. It may be that in some sense we finally *see* the world in different ways. Even when two things in different cultures look alike their apparent similarity may mask profound differences. And some things in all cultures are extremely hard to eradicate—religion (above all—Gao Xingjian admits the "worship of idols by atheists"[8]), the forbidden power of sexuality, obscure ontological divergences, and so on.

In his "Translator's Preface" to the notoriously obscure *I Ching: The Book of Changes*, written in Oxford in 1882, long after he had left China, James Legge, a missionary and sinologist who has appeared frequently in the pages of this book, writes of his developing sense, realized over many years of reflection, of how to translate from Chinese into English. His first translation of the *I Ching* was made in 1854, and there, he recalls, he first attempted a "literal" rendering of the original. This, he admits, resulted in a translation that was, to all intents and purposes, unintelligible. He came to realize only later that the very different natures of Chinese and English made any such literal translation simply impossible:

> The written characters of the Chinese are not representations of words, but symbols of ideas, and . . . the combination of them in composition is not a representation of what the writer would say, but of what he thinks. It is vain therefore for a translator to attempt a literal translation.[9]

For the translator into English from the Chinese, Legge thus maintains:

> When the symbolic characters have brought his mind en rapport with that of the author, he is free to render the ideas in his own or any other speech in the best manner he can attain to. This is the rule which Mencius followed in interpreting the old poems of his country: "We must try with our thoughts to meet the scope of a sentence and then we shall apprehend it."[10]

8. Gao Xingjian, *Soul Mountain*, 454.
9. Legge, "Translator's Preface," xcv.
10. Legge, "Translator's Preface," xcv.

Of course, something very complicated is going on here. We are reading an ancient Chinese sage, Mencius, in translation as he is writing about the translation of ancient Chinese poems from an earlier culture. Mencius is here translated into English by a European scholar in order to illustrate the difficulties of translation from the pictographic script of Chinese into a European language.

Our own conversations in the present book also have had their complications as must be evident to every reader. As a dialogue between China and the West they are woefully one-sided, being between a Chinese scholar with excellent English, and a British scholar with almost no Chinese language at all. Each struggles to interpret texts that lie far outside his own culture and history. Furthermore, even between very good friends the cultural differences remain, and we have spent hours trying to understand words and concepts that seem, ultimately, to defy translation. Ou Guang-an has recently published a book (this one written, by a Chinese scholar, in English and published in China) entitled *Classical and Modern Chinese: Case Studies of English-Chinese Translation in Modern China* (2017) in which the primary theoretical foundations are provided by a Western scholar, George Steiner, and his book *After Babel: Aspects of Language and Translation* (Second edition, 1992) which is almost entirely concerned with translations between *European* languages. Does the nature of Chinese introduce new issues and problems? In 1993, David Jasper, the other of the present authors, edited a book of essays entitled *Translating Religious Texts*, with a Foreword by none other than George Steiner, which concludes with a reference to "the enduring parable of necessary unknowing at the heart of translation." And yet that "necessary unknowing" lies at the very heart of all speech.[11]

But it is clear that we cannot stop there. Ou Guang-an appropriates Steiner's fourfold "hermeneutic motion" in his studies of the translations from English poetry of Wu Mi (into classical Chinese) and Mu Dan (into modern Chinese). The translator, says Steiner, must begin with trust, a gesture of "radical generosity."[12] But then after initial trust comes aggression, and Steiner writes that "the second move of the translator is incursive and extractive." After this, the third move is incorporative, an importation of meaning, and finally the fourth stage is the restoration of balance to compensate for the imbalance, balancing the risk that is involved in the initial act of trust.

11. Steiner, "Foreword," x–xiv.
12. Steiner, *After Babel*, 312.

But we are not sure that this description entirely represents our experience in our exercises in this book—a European reading Chinese texts and theology and a Chinese reader engaging with texts from English and biblical literature. Communication there has been, but even in friendship it is always on edge and always risky. What Steiner calls that "necessary unknowing" is an endlessly destabilizing element between cultures, and we suspect that at heart, and finally, there is in some sense a religious element in this.

Religion has haunted all of our conversations and the texts—ever present and ever inaccessible, hard to pin down, whether we like it or not. In Gao Xingjian's *Soul Mountain*, the traveler (the novelist?) meets a Buddhist Master who had "for some reason" "wanted to convert to Catholicism." But then, "One day he came to a sudden realization—the Pope was far away in the West and inaccessible, so he might as well rely on Buddha."[13] Is that, then, the nature of our religion—it being rooted simply in its cultural and local availability? All else, quite apart from any questions of truth, is simply inaccessible. And in modern literature, religion is often the grit in the oyster—to be abandoned and trampled upon by secular ideologies, but never quite absent, never quite subdued.

Is this why Ou Guang-an goes back to the biblical book of Job, perhaps our earliest theological debate in the West on the mystery and nature of God? Or is this why David Jasper seeks to understand the nature of Lu Xun's soul searching for the salvation of the Chinese people? The European Christian missionaries of the nineteenth century engaged in what was known as the Term Question. This was an attempt to find an answer to the question as to which Chinese term might be most appropriately used to express the biblical sense of "God." But by what means can such appropriateness be judged? James Legge suggested parallels and even more between Confucius and the prophets of the Hebrew Bible—and for his biblical embracing of Chinese culture he was finally sent home to England, his missionary career at an end. The same thing had happened to Matteo Ricci centuries before.

But we wonder if, in the end, those conservative missionaries were actually right about the Term Question. Although their methods and attitudes were often profoundly attractive, yet we are deeply uneasy about their universal conclusion. Every "god," in the end it seems, is steadfastly culturally exclusive. A recent book by Jenny Wong, a Chinese scholar who

---

13. Gao Xingjian, *Soul Mountain*, 279.

gained her doctorate in Britain, is entitled *The Translatability of the Religious Dimension in Shakespeare* (2018). She is certainly correct to concentrate on social, political, and cultural elements rather than simply linguistic difficulties in the examination of the process (or often omission) of rendering Shakespeare's religious terms into Chinese. Often, strictly these elements and words are simply untranslatable, rendering the exercise in inevitable cultural imbalance. There can be no conclusion. Wong explores the case study of *The Merchant of Venice* and how its biblical allusions play with religious terms and finally the character of Shylock—a figure deeply rooted in European and Christian cultural and theological prejudices and stereotypes of the Jew. Yet what becomes clear at the same time is that the power of religion remains present in translation, though often turned into quite different social or political references. Wong concludes that, in some form, the power of religion, even when belief is absent, is almost un-eradicable and that "even the state can rarely compete with religion in terms of the intensity of its authority for society as a whole."[14]

Returning to our own conversations that we have been engaged with in this book it has been clear that "religion" is present everywhere even where this is neither deliberate nor conscious. It is also apparent that the word "religion" is very difficult to pin down or define, especially in intercultural conversations. This is not merely that it is "lost in translation," but we are forced to conclude that the old European adage, promoted by some early sinologists like Herbert Giles,[15] that China is a culture without religion, is patently not the case, though whether that term can be precisely translated between the culture of the Christian West and China is, at best, highly problematical. Contemporary Chinese scholars like Yang Huilin have thrown cold water over the claims of some European scholars that there are deep similarities between early Christianity and Mao Zedong's teachings,[16] though Christian visitors to Mao's birthplace in Shaoshan, Hunan Province, cannot fail to be uncomfortably aware of the reminiscences of Christ's nativity in the stable-like environment of the Chairman's birth. And the link between literature, culture and religion is unavoidable and has been at the heart of all the conversations in this book. If the presentation of Mao Zedong's life and teachings attract uneasy associations with those of Jesus in the gospels, it is true also that in Ou Guang-an's university in

---

14. Wong, *Translatability*, 277. See also Ramet, "Sacred Values," 3–20.
15. See, for example, Giles, *History of Chinese Literature*.
16. Yang Huilin, *China, Christianity, and the Question of Culture*, 40–41.

Shihezi in Xingjiang, China, a stone carving of the head of William Shakespeare stands serenely next to the a similar carving of Mao Zedong. Culture, literature and religion cannot in the end be separated.

And yet in the end any precise *translation* between languages and cultures, it may be, is strictly impossible even if necessary. At best, if we follow George Steiner's four-stage model of translation, it involves moments of violence, invasion and appropriation that require healing and restoration in an "enactment of reciprocity." In translation, Steiner asserts:

> We encircle and invade cognitively. We come home laden, and thus again off-balance, having caused disequilibrium throughout the system by taking away from "the other" and by adding, though possibly with ambiguous consequence, to our own. The system is now off-tilt. The hermeneutic must compensate. If it is to be authentic, it must mediate into exchange and restored parity.[17]

In our conversations, after a growing friendship had shed niceties and allowed us to become more properly critical and honest with one another, we found the disturbing, even violent quality of Steiner's words to be true—all that language of encirclement and invasion, of appropriating and owning—and perhaps this was necessarily so and as part of the growth in understanding between us. Here something must become *mine* before it can again become *ours*. But that cannot be the end of it and understanding, conversation and friendship begin and grow, like literature itself, in the simple, *universal* stuff of everyday life and being. As Klaus Klostermeier, writing in a suspension between German and Indian cultures, once wrote:

> Everyday life is in many respects the same everywhere—one meets good people and not so good ones, friendly and unfriendly ones, some that are diligent and others that are lazy, fat ones and thin ones, gay people and sad people, honest ones and dishonest ones, the pious and the Pharisees, mockers and fanatics, people who are to be taken seriously and others whose thinking is confused, silent ones and gossips.[18]

As the fabled Dubliner once said of James Joyce's *Ulysses*, "we're all in the bloody book." And of Joyce's *Finnegans Wake* (1939) we might say the same as the "narrator" in *Soul Mountain*—"This isn't a novel!"[19] But they—

---

17. Steiner, *After Babel*, 316.
18. Klostermeier, *Hindu and Christian in Vrindaban*, 88.
19. Gao Xingjian, *Soul Mountain*, 452.

we—are all there in the text dealing with eating, sex, loneliness, friendship, all of us living in a world that is both vanishing and ever coming into being.

Perhaps there is something Irish at the heart of our conversations—prompting one of us, a Chinese scholar, to devote so much research time to the poetry of W. B. Yeats. Or perhaps it is just that true conversation and friendship are finally universal, overcoming untranslatable differences between language, religion and cultures that remain steadfastly different, but finally acknowledging a deeper and fundamentally human commonality.

14

Final Remarks

Ou Guang-an

THIS BOOK HAS THROUGHOUT been in the form of a conversation—between two cultures and between two friends each trying to read the literature of the other. It seems appropriate therefore that each of us has a final word from our own perspective. But this is not to deny that underlying all differences there is a deeper and fundamentally human commonality. Language and even ideas may sometimes be untranslatable but even such gaps in our mutual understanding may be less significant than the universality of the human spirit.

Yes! "Steadfast difference" and "human commonality" are exactly the expressions I am looking for—although I have been studying English for a quarter of a century I realize, sadly, that my vocabulary escapes me so often and I am still in an impossible situation in pinning down the right expression when needed.

Certainly on the journey of this conversation "difference" is something we encountered regularly, and sometimes in such an unexpected way that it seemed to hit a crucial blow on what we, or at least I, took for granted before. When David read chapter 72 of Gao Xingjian's novel *Soul Mountain*, a chapter which is totally different from other parts of the novel and which itself is already different enough from other works in 1980s' China, his immediate response was that in George Eliot's novel *Adam Bede* there is a similar chapter. This did not immediately come to my mind even though I had read *Adam Bede*. However, when David was pondering why Gao Xingjian suddenly interrupted the narration and inserted a chapter (the aforementioned chapter 72) that discusses the nature of a novel, I immediately thought of the Monkey King (whose real name is Wu Kong, meaning "realization of emptiness") in the classical Chinese novel *Journey to the West*, because seventy-two is the number of times that the Monkey King can transform himself.

My guess is that Gao Xingjian harbors an intention to engender some change in the form of the Chinese novel here and he did indeed make that change. Not only does the content of chapter 72 seem to be irrelevant to the whole novel, but also near to the end of the chapter there is a long passage that has no punctuation, a phenomenon which is seldom observed in modern Chinese writing but in which it is also easy to discern the influence of the last chapter of James Joyce's *Ulysses*. In consideration of Gao's educational background, taking French as his major in college, Joyce's influence would not be too difficult to grasp. Other similar examples of writing drawing on elements in the Western tradition can be found in the work of contemporary Chinese novelists. For example, Mo Yan himself has readily acknowledged the influence of William Faulkner and García Márquez and one only has to look at some of his "Red Sorghum" series of writings (including short stories and novels) to detect that the narration centering around a certain township in Mo Yan's work raises prompt echoes from Faulkner's "Jefferson" novels (named as Yoknapatawpha County). These two examples of literary influence from Western writers, in general terms, on Chinese novelists show a seemingly paradoxical but undeniable fact that in the modern context the cultural flow between western regions and oriental regions is mostly one-sided, intellectual traffic being very largely from the west to the east. And that is probably one of the fundamental reasons why a Chinese scholar should publish an English book in China.

Today the study of foreign languages and literatures is still one of the most popular academic fields in Chinese colleges, universities, and places of higher education. English language and literature department Ph. D candidates usually write their graduating thesis in English and after graduation they are likely to publish their work with, or without, necessary and appropriate revisions. Their counterpart candidates in Chinese departments also pursue research in foreign languages and literatures, usually under the title of Comparative Literature, and some of them also prefer to write and publish in English. This is still a major element in the work of Chinese scholars who wish to gain standing with the larger international academic community. In this respect Chinese scholars in scientific fields do much better than scholars in the humanities and arts and even social sciences. Publication in English is almost a necessity.

Final Remarks | Guang-an

For me, to investigate into the possibility and significance of translating English works into classical Chinese, in the case of Wu Mi, is the result of deep reflection. Born and raised into a traditional culture, Wu Mi (1894–1978) was one of the earliest scholars of comparative literature in China and also a distinguished poet. He received a traditional Chinese education before he was accepted by Tsinghua College in Beijing (later Tsinghua University), then a preparatory institution for Chinese students to study abroad. It was paradoxically, established through the refund, to the then government, of compensation paid to the United States for defeat in the Siege of the International Legations in 1900. In Tsinghua School, and later in the Universities of Virginia and Harvard Wu Mi also received a systematic Western education, mainly in the disciplines of literature and philosophy and under the influence of such prominent contemporary philosophers as Irving Babbitt. But, as a result of the solid traditional education which he received in his childhood and youth, Wu Mi chose to translate foreign works in comparatively strict classical Chinese, an attitude in direct opposition to such major proponents of modern Chinese as the philosopher Hu Shi (1891–1962), who attended Columbia University for doctoral study as a beneficiary of the same refund as Wu Mi. To some extent, when facing the shift of Western ideas (literature, philosophy, arts, economics, and so on) into modern China, Hu Shi's attitude was more radical, earning him a nickname—the backbone of "total westernization," dedicated to the employment or copying of everything from the West. Wu Mi and others, alternatively, argued that while on the one hand we should learn from the West, on the other hand traditional Chinese culture should not be cut down or deleted abruptly. The magazine, *The Critical Review*, founded by Wu Mi and others who held similar ideas published both translations of foreign works and works written in traditional forms and these translations were rendered in classical Chinese, which was the major tool for literary writing before the New Cultural Movement in 1919. Then the essential question became apparent: can a work of foreign literature, say a Shakespeare sonnet, be rightly rendered into classical Chinese, a form employed by Li Bai and Du Fu? However, in the course of time, the voices of Wu Mi and his school gradually diminished after the 1930s and it was not until the 1980s that they were again taken up into serious academic consideration. In the 1920s even Lu Xun was highly critical of the *Critical Review* school.

On February 1 1922, in the supplement of the *Morning Post* Lu Xun published a pungent criticism of proposals of the *Critical Review* school with the title "Evaluation on *The Critical Review*," stating that members of that school were not proficient in old scholarship (traditional Chinese learning) but neither were they qualified in introducing the new one (the learning from the West). To a certain extent, Lu Xun's reputation rests on his strong, sometimes even harsh, criticism of his fellow countrymen such as is narrated in *The Real Story of Ah-Q*. In the revolutionary context, such criticism was hailed as a call for revolutionary actions, and thus the title of Lu Xun's first collection of short stories was officially translated as *Call to Arms*, while in the English world it is usually rendered as *Outcry*. It is here that we find the famous passage, so often referred to in this book, when he turns to literature to save the spirit of the Chinese people

As is noted in some translations the change which Lu Xun wanted to bring about is rendered as to "soul" instead of "spirit." The semantic difference between the two words here does not matter because the intention of Lu Xun is obvious enough: if China at that time can be compared to a man, then he is a man weak in spirit if not in body. So to save such a weak man the most important task is to change and cheer his spirit. However, no matter which specific word is employed, the sense and idea of salvation is something that is absent in traditional Chinese history and culture. If, from a certain perspective, we agree that by saying that he intends to change his countrymen's spirit Lu Xun means to "save" his country by saving his countrymen's spirit first, then, we should take other things into consideration. That is, although equipped with a formal traditional Chinese education Lu Xun later came under the influence of new learning, that is Western scholarship, in his middle school years and more importantly from his years of study in Japan. And Japan in the early years of the twentieth century was coming increasingly under the influence of Western culture and intellectual thought, including the Greek and Christian traditions. Therefore, when Lu Xun was writing was he also reflecting on the word of literature as an agent for salvation, a Western concept, though the idea of the opposition between body and spirit was not unfamiliar in Chinese culture? Nothing is ever straightforward in Lu Xun's writing. Reading him raises simultaneously both senses of fragmentation and uneasiness, especially for a Chinese reader. As scholars would argue:

> Like Adorno, Lu Xun is concerned with the "truth content" of art, which is not to be found in narratives of harmony and

reconciliation; rather, it is manifested in art's ability to mirror the internal contradictions and antagonistic state of the world.[1]

Interestingly, recent years have witnessed a somewhat heated debate in Chinese intellectual circles in the investigation of Lu Xun's work in translating from other languages, another legacy, along with his short stories and critical articles which shows a great deal of Western influence. Again it is interesting to note that some of Lu Xun's early translation and writings, especially his academic writings, are done in classical Chinese. Then how did the "classical" Lu Xun become such a major figure in modern Chinese cultural movements? At times he seems a deeply divided figure. In some respects there seems to be a straight dividing line between Lu Xun's classical Chinese writing and his modern Chinese writing penned after the influence of the New Culture Movement. However, when we read his middle or later writings, outside any scholarly critical perspective, we would feel no unfamiliarity or estrangement in such passages as the one quoted above. The understanding and appreciation of what Lu Xun means by changing his countrymen's spirit or soul would just be natural, even though the question of salvation, drawn mostly from Western culture, lingers on.

The natural process of understanding something which may come from Western culture in a modern Chinese novel or short story is not difficult to find. *Fortress Besieged* (1947), a novel by Qian Zhongshu, one of the most prominent students of Wu Mi, is just such an example. In the novel, there is a scene when several characters are discussing the question of marriage, and one pompous character brags about his relationship with the British philosopher Bertrand Russell (this character calls Russell "Bertie"). When he admonished "Bertie" on his several attempts at marriage and divorce the philosopher replied by quoting a saying, that marriage is like a gilded cage; the birds outside want to fly into it while those inside want to fly out. Then one of the two female protagonists replies that in French there is also a similar saying; only it is not about a cage but a fortress, *forteresse assiégée*, that is, people outside the fortress want to rush into it while those inside want to flee out.[2] When reading such similes or metaphors, even with the clear indication that they are from either English or French, a Chinese reader does not find it so strange or eccentric, because, in the terms of the Swiss linguist Ferdinand de Saussure, the signified would be the same, and only the signifiers are different. The practice and reflection

1. Cheng, *Literary Remains*, 13.
2. Qian Zhongshu, *Fortress Besieged*, 89.

on communicating Chinese literature and Western literature for Qian Zhongshu can be summarized in two sentences which appear in the preface to his masterpiece on literary criticism *On the Art of Poetry*:

> East or west, the psychology could be the same;
> South or north, learnings play a similar game.
> (東海西海，心理攸同；南學北學，道術未裂。)³

For such an acute observer as Qian Zhongshu, when the western influence on oriental culture (China included) is so obvious, the influence of Chinese literature on Western literature is also not going to be missed. After studying in Oxford University and reading avidly in the Bodleian Library (which Qian described in a rather interesting translation as 飽蠹樓, sounding something like the word Bodleian but literally meaning "tower full of bookworm bitten wood"),⁴ Qian Zhongshu wrote a thesis, published only posthumously, which discusses the image of China in English literature—*China in the English Literature of the Seventeenth and Eighteenth Centuries*.⁵ The acute awareness of Qian Zhongshu can also be found echoed in David's three essays, but especially in the essay on Sino-Christian theology.

---

3. Qian Zhongshu, "Preface," 1. *On the Art of Poetry* was first published in 1948 but it was not until the end of the 1970s that Qian decided to make additions and revisions. There are two books by Qian Zhongshu that are always printed in classical Chinese characters: one is *On the Art of Poetry* and the other is *Limited Views: Essays on Ideas and Letters*, probably because both of them were written in elegant classical Chinese. The classical Chinese characters are also used here in the quotation. There are other similar sayings by Qian Zhongshu as quoted here—for instance, "The underlying principle is one, but its apportionments are many (理一分殊)"; "the quality is the same, but feelings toward the quality vary (名同分異)"; and so on—which shows Qian's idea that "the initial unsuspected affinity gives way to appreciation of diversity amid general topic or type." See Qian Zhongshu, "Introduction," 18.

4. Although Qian Zhongshu himself translated very little of Western works, his translation, scattered fragmentally in various writings, is considered pertinent in meaning, fluent in expression, and elegant in literary feature. With limited space in this book, our conversations do not touch specifically upon the topic of translation. And yet, however highly we praise the essential role played by translation in cultural communication is not enough, as Zhang Longxi, a contemporary renowned scholar who is also influenced greatly by Qian Zhongshu, expresses: "When two cultures meet in their first encounters, translation, however difficult, faulty, and inadequate, constitutes the necessary first step towards mutual understanding, an indispensible bridge crossing over the gaping linguistic and cultural difference" (Zhang Longxi, "Introduction," 11).

5. Tang Yan, *Qian Zhongshu*, 101. Qian was planning to write on the topic of "The Influence of Chinese Literature on English Literature" but the proposal was rejected by his advisor at Oxford University.

Final Remarks | Guang-an

David's worrying about the future and indeed the nature of Sino-Christian theology is definitely not without cause. What will appear exactly after, say a decade or two, when Christian theology, which is profoundly rooted in the thought and forms of Greek philosophical reflection within the Christian tradition, encounters a remarkably different cultural context in which Confucianism occupies a predominant position, is hard to assess precisely. Nevertheless, it is this acute worrying that brings something that truly effects an everlasting influence on academic, or more specifically, cultural communication. The tension goes back to the nineteenth century and to James Legge when he puzzled his London audience in his lectures that were later published as *The Religions of China* (1880).

A particular point needs to be mentioned here before we finally conclude. When David and I were reflecting and writing about the book of Job and *Zhuangzi* we both felt, in some way, interested in the concept of "doing nothing"—*wu wei*—in Daoism. In Daoism, Dao is also the "way," or the "great way," the beginning of everything, as narrated in the *Daodejing*:

> The great Way floods her banks; she can go left or right.
> She completes her tasks, pursues her affairs, yet she is given no ownership for this.
> The myriad things flow back to her, yet she does not lord it over them.[6]

Here "myriad things" more literally in the original Chinese means "all things." The great Way "floods" or "flows" any way it wishes and one has to perceive it rather than to "touch" it. Similarly, in scripture, the wind blows wherever it wants to blow, one does not know where it comes from and where it goes and one only hears the voice (John 3:8). The Way and Wind is the very name of the place in the Hong Kong Special Administrative Region—Tao Fong Shan—where all these friendly yet thought-provoking cross-cultural conversations began.

---

6. Laozi, *Daodejing*, 71.

Suggested Further Reading

Intercultural Studies

Jasper, David, Geng Youzhuang, and Wang Hai, eds. *A Poetics of Translation: Between Chinese and English Literature*. Waco, TX: Baylor University Press, 2016.
Spence, Jonathan D. *The Chan's Great Continent: China in Western Minds*. New York: Norton, 1998.
Yang Huilin. *China, Christianity, and the Question of Culture*. Waco, TX: Baylor University Press, 2014.
Zhang Longxi. *From Comparison to World Literature*. New York: State University of New York Press, 2015.
———. *The Tao and the Logos: Literary Hermeneutics, East and West*. Durham, NC: Duke University Press, 1992.

Religion and Christianity in China

Arthur, Shawn. *Contemporary Religions in China*. London: Routledge, 2019.
Lai, Pan-Chui, and Jason Lam, eds. *Sino-Christian Theology: A Theological Qua Cultural Movement in Contemporary China*. Frankfurt: Peter Lang, 2010.
Starr, Chloë. *Chinese Theology: Text and Context*. New Haven: Yale University Press, 2016.

Journals

Christianity and Literature 68.1 (2018). Special Issue, "Christianity and Chinese Literary Studies." Edited by Sharon Kim and Chloë Starr. Published by the Conference on Christianity and Literature.
Journal for the Study of Christian Culture, Western Marxism, and Theology. Published in Chinese by the Institute for the Study of Christian Culture, Renmin University of China, Beijing.
Literature and Religion. Published in English by the Korean Society for Literature and Religion.
Literature and Theology 28.2 (2014). Special Issue, "China and the West in Dialogue." Edited by David Jasper and Wang Hai. Published by Oxford University Press.
Yearbook of Chinese Theology. Edited by Paulos Z. Huang. Published by Brill.

Literature and Religion

The writing of Lu Xun has figured largely in our conversations in this book. An excellent English translation of his fiction is now available as a Penguin Classic:

Lu Xun. *The Real Story of Ah-Q and Other Tales of China: The Complete Fiction of Lu Xun*. Translated by Julia Lovell. Harmondsworth: Penguin, 2009.

Bibliography

Aeschylus. *The Complete Plays of Aeschylus (Translated into English Rhyming Verse with Commentaries and Notes)*. Translated by Gilbert Murray. London: George Allen & Unwin, 1952.
Aesop. *Aesop's Fables*. Translated by V. S. Vernon Jones. Ware: Wordsworth Editions, 1994.
Archibald, Douglas. *Yeats*. Syracuse: Syracuse University Press, 1983.
Auberbach, Erich. "Odysseus's Scar." In *Mimesis*, by Erich Auberbach, 3–23. Translated by Willard R. Trask. Princeton: Princeton University Press, 1968.
Bakhtin, Mikhail. *The Dialogic Imagination*. Edited by Michael Holquist. Translated by Caryl Emerson and Michael Holquist. Austin: University of Texas Press, 1981.
———. "Problems of Dostoevsky's Poetics: Polyphony and Unfinalizability." In vol. 5 of *Complete Works of Bahktin*, translated by Bai Chunren et al., 1–573. Shijiazhuang: Hebei Education, 1998.
Barnhart, Robert K., ed. *The Barnhart Dictionary of Etymology*. New York: H. W. Wilson, 1988.
Bell, Vereen M. *Yeats and the Logic of Formalism*. Columbia: University of Missouri Press, 2006.
Bellah, Robert N. *Religion in Human Evolution*. Cambridge, MA: Harvard University Press, 2011.
Bew, Paul. *Ireland: The Politics of Enmity 1789–2006*. Oxford History of Modern Europe. Oxford: Oxford University Press, 2007.
Bian Zhilin. *New Collection of Bian Zhilin's Works*. Beijing: People's Literature, 2009.
Blanchot, Maurice. *The Space of Literature*. Translated by Ann Smock. Lincoln: University of Nebraska Press, 1982.
Bloom, Harold. *Yeats*. New York: Oxford University Press, 1970.
Boethius. *The Consolation of Philosophy*. Translated by V. E. Watts. Harmondsworth: Penguin, 1969.
Bradley, Anthony. *Imagining Ireland in the Poems and Plays of W. B. Yeats: Nation, Class, and State*. New York: Palgrave Macmillan, 2011.
Brooks, Cleanth. *The Well Wrought Urn: Studies in the Structure of Poetry*. New York: Mainer, 1956.
Brown, Terrence. *The Life of W. B. Yeats: A Critical Biography*. Hoboken: Wiley Blackwell, 1999.
Cao Xueqin, and Gao E. *A Dream of Red Mansions*. 4 vols. Translated by Yang Xianyi and Gladys Yang. Beijing: Foreign Languages, 2008.

Bibliography

Chaucer, Geoffrey. *The Works*. Edited by F. N. Robinson. London: Oxford University Press, 1957.

Chen Guying. *Contemporary Annotation and Translation of Zhuangzi*. Beijing: Commercial, 2007.

Cheng, Eileen J. *Literary Remains: Death, Trauma, and Lu Xun's Refusal to Mourn*. Honolulu: University of Hawaii Press, 2013

The Chinese Study Bible. Shanghai: Chinese Christian Association, 2006.

Chow, Alexander. *Chinese Public Theology: Generational Shifts and Confucian Imagination in Chinese Christianity*. Oxford: Oxford University Press, 2018.

———. *Theosis, Sino-Christian Theology, and the Second Chinese Enlightenment*. London: Palgrave Macmillan, 2013.

Chuang Tzu. *The Complete Works of Chuang Tzu*. Translated by Burton Watson. New York: Columbia University Press, 1968.

———. *The Inner Chapters*. Translated by Solala Towler. London: Watkins, 2010.

Confucius. *The Analects*. Translated by D. C. Lau. London: Penguin, 1979.

———. *The Analects*. Translated by Arthur Waley. Beijing: Foreign Language Teaching and Research, 1998.

———. *The Analects of Confucius*. Translated by William Edward Soothill. Yokohama: Fukuin, 1910.

———. *The Analects of Confucius*. Translated by Chichung Huang. New York: Oxford University Press, 1997.

———. *The Analects of Confucius: A Philosophical Translation*. Translated by Roger T. Ames and Henry Rosemont Jr. New York: Random, 1999.

———. *Confucian Analects*. Vol. 1 of *The Chinese Classics*. Translated by James Legge. Hong Kong: At the Author's, 1861.

———. *Confucian Analects*. Vol. 1 of *The Chinese Classics: With a Translation, Critical and Exegetical Notes, Prolegomena, and Copious Indexes*. Translated by James Legge. Taipei: Royal, 1983.

Crenshaw, James L. "Job." In *The Oxford Bible Commentary*, edited by John Barton and John Muddiman, 331–55. Oxford: Oxford University Press, 2001.

Criveller, Gianni. *Wan Ming Jidu lun [Preaching Christ during the Late Ming Dynasty]*. Translated by Wang Qi. Chengdu: Sichuan People, 1999.

Culler, Jonathan. *Structuralist Poetics: Structuralism, Linguistics, and the Study of Literature*. London: Routledge & Kegan Paul, 1975.

Cullingford, Elizabeth. *Yeats, Ireland, and Fascism*. New York: New York University Press, 1981.

Davies, Gloria. *Lu Xun's Revolution: Writing in a Time of Violence*. Cambridge, MA: Harvard University Press, 2013.

Der-Wei Wang, David. "Chinese Literature from 1841 to 1937." In *From 1375*, edited by Kang-I Sun Chang and Stephen Owen, 413–564. Vol. 2 of *The Cambridge History of Chinese Literature*. Cambridge: Cambridge University Press, 2010.

Ding Bingwei. "Memory Recovery and History Reconstruction: Analysis on The Wanderings of Oisin." *World Literature Review* 2 (2007) 133–34.

Drabble, Margaret, ed. *The Genius of Thomas Hardy*. London: Weidenfeld and Nicolson, 1976.

Eagleton, Terry. *Culture and the Death of God*. New Haven: Yale University Press, 2015.

Ebrey, Patricia Buckley. *The Cambridge Illustrated History of China*. 2nd ed. Cambridge: Cambridge University Press, 2010.

Bibliography

Eliot, George. *Adam Bede*. n.p., 1859.
Ellmann, Richard. *The Identity of Yeats*. Stanford: Stanford University Press, 1968.
———. *Yeats: The Man and the Masks*. London: Macmillan, 1949.
Fisher, Joe. *The Hidden Hardy*. London: Macmillan, 1992.
Foster, R. F. *Yeats: A Life*. 2 vols. Oxford: Oxford University Press, 1997, 2003.
Foucault, Michel. *The Hermeneutics of the Subject: Lectures at the Collège de France, 1981–1982*. Translated by Graham Burchell. New York: Picador, 2006.
———. *The History of Sexuality*. Vol. 1. Translated by Robert Hurley. Harmondsworth: Penguin, 1976.
———. *On the Government of the Living*. Edited by Michel Senellart. Translated by Graham Burchell. New York: Picador, 2012.
Franke, William. *A Theology of Literature*. Eugene, OR: Cascade, 2017.
Fu Hao. "Christian Elements in Yeats's Works." *Foreign Literature* 6 (2008) 14–21.
———. *Yeats*. Hangzhou: Zhejiang People's, 1997.
Gadamer, Hans-Georg. *Zhe xue quan shi xue [Philosophical Hermeneutics]*. Translated by Xia Zhenping. Shanghai: Shanghai Translations, 1998.
Gao Xingjian. *Soul Mountain*. Translated by Mabel Lee. London: Harper Perennial, 2004.
Geng Youzhuang. *Between East and West: Word and Image*. Waco, TX: Baylor University Press, 2016.
Giles, Herbert. *A History of Chinese Literature*. London: William Heinemann, 1901.
———. *The Travels of Fa-hsien*. Cambridge: Cambridge University Press, 1923.
Girardot, Norman J. *The Victorian Translation of China: James Legge's Oriental Pilgrimage*. Berkeley: University of California Press, 2002.
Goode, John. *Thomas Hardy: The Offensive Truth*. Oxford: Basil Blackwell, 1988.
Graves, Robert. *The Greek Myths*. Vol. 1. Harmondsworth: Penguin, 1955.
Gutiérrez, Gustavo. *Essential Writings*. Edited by James B. Nickoloff. London: SCM, 1996.
Hall, James, and Martin Steinmann, eds. *The Permanence of Yeats*. New York: Macmillan, 1950.
Hardy, Florence Emily. *The Later Years of Thomas Hardy, 1892–1928*. London: Macmillan, 1930.
———. *The Later Years of Thomas Hardy, 1892–1928*. London: Studio Editions, 1994.
———. *Life of Thomas Hardy*. London: Macmillan, 1962.
Hardy, Thomas. *The Dynasts*. n.p., 1908.
———. *Jude the Obscure*. n.p., 1895.
———. *The Mayor of Casterbridge*. n.p., 1886.
———. *Tess of the D'Urbervilles*. Translated by Sun Fa-li. Nanking: Yilin, 2015.
———. *Tess of the D'Urbervilles*. Translated by Wu Di. Shanghai: Shanghai Literature and Art, 2016.
———. *Tess of the D'Urbervilles: An Authoritative Text; Hardy and the Novel; Criticism*. Edited by Scott Elledge. New York: Norton, 1965.
———. *Tess of the D'Urbervilles (Library Edition)*. London: Macmillan, 1949.
———. *Tess of the D'Urbervilles: A Pure Woman*. Translated by Zhang Guruo. Beijing: People's Literature, 2018.
Hašek, Jaroslav. *The Good Soldier Švejk and His Fortunes in the World War*. Translated by Cecil Parrott. 1921. Reprint, Harmondsworth: Penguin, 1974.
Henn, T. R. *The Bible as Literature*. London: Lutterworth, 1970.
———. *The Harvest of Tragedy*. London: Methuen, 1966.
———. *The Lonely Tower: Studies in the Poetry of W. B. Yeats*. London: Methuen, 1950.

Bibliography

———. *The Lonely Tower: Studies in the Poetry of W. B. Yeats*. 2nd ed. London: Methuen, 1965.
Holdeman, David. *The Cambridge Introduction to W. B. Yeats*. Shanghai: Shanghai Foreign Language Education, 2008.
Holdeman, David, and Ben Levitas, eds. *W. B. Yeats in Context*. Cambridge: Cambridge University Press, 2010.
Homer. *The Odyssey*. Translated by E. V. Rieu. Harmondsworth: Penguin, 1946.
Horner, Robyn. "Translator's Introduction." In *In Excess: Studies of Saturated Phenomena*, by Jean-Luc Marion, ix–xx. Translated by Robyn Hormer. New York: Fordham University Press, 2002.
Howes, Marjorie. *Yeats's Nation: Gender, Class, and Irishness*. Cambridge: Cambridge University Press, 1996.
James, Edwin O. *Comparative Religion*. London: Methuen, 1961.
Jasper, David. *Heaven in Ordinary: Poetry and Religion in a Secular Age*. Cambridge: Lutterworth, 2018.
———. "Reflections on the Maturity of Religion and Theology in Literature: A Cultural Dialogue." *Christianity and Literature* 68.1 (2018) 131–40.
———. Review of *From Comparison to World Literature*, by Zhang Longxi. *Literature and Theology* 31.1 (2017) 121–23.
Jasper, David, Geng Youzhuang, and Wang Hai, eds. *A Poetics of Translation: Between Chinese and English Literature*. Waco: Baylor University Press, 2016.
Jeffares, Norman. *A Commentary on the Collected Poems of W. B. Yeats*. Stanford: Stanford University Press, 1968.
———. *A New Commentary on the Collected Poems of W. B. Yeats*. London: Macmillan, 1968.
———. *W. B. Yeats: Man and Poet*. 3rd ed. London: Palgrave Macmillan, 1996.
———. *W. B. Yeats: A New Biography*. New York: Continuum International, 2001.
Jones, Andrew F. "Afterword." In *Chronicle of a Blood Merchant*, by Yu Hua, 253–63. Translated by Andrew F. Jones. New York: Anchor, 2004.
Josipovici, Gabriel. *The Book of God: A Response to the Bible*. New Haven: Yale University Press, 1988.
Jung, Carl Gustav. *Answer to Job*. Translated by R. F. C. Hull. London: Hodder and Stoughton, 1965.
Kam Louie. "Defining Modern Chinese Culture." In *The Cambridge Companion to Modern Chinese Culture*, edited by Kam Louie, 1–19. Cambridge: Cambridge University Press, 2008.
Kelly, John. *A W. B. Yeats Chronology*. New York: Palgrave Macmillan, 2003.
Kerenyi, Carl. *The Gods of the Greeks*. London: Thames and Hudson, 1961.
Kern, Martin. "Early Chinese Literature, Beginnings through Western Han." In vol. 1 of *The Cambridge History of Chinese Literature*, edited by Kang-I Sun Chang and Stephen Owen, 1–115. Cambridge: Cambridge University Press, 2010.
Klostermeier, Klaus. *Hindu and Christian in Vrindaban*. Translated by Antonia Fonseca. London: SCM, 1969.
Knight, G. Wilson. *The Wheel of Fire: Interpretations of Shakespearian Tragedy*. 1930. Reprint, London: Methuen, 1969.
Lao-Tze. *Lao-Tze in English Version from the Chinese*. Translated by Francis F. Y. Chang (张发榕). Taiwan: Published by the translator, 1984.
Lao Tzu. *Tao Te Ching*. Translated by D. C. Lau. Harmondsworth: Penguin Books, 1963.

BIBLIOGRAPHY

———. *Tao Te Ching*. Translated by Arthur Waley. Beijing: Foreign Languages Teaching and Research, 1998.
Laozi. *Daodejing*. Translated by Edmund Ryden. Oxford: Oxford University Press, 2008.
Lardreau, Guy, Christian Lambert, and Peter Hebblethwaite. *The Christian-Marxist Dialogue*. London: DLT, 1977.
Larkin, Philip. *The North Ship*. 1945. Reprint, London: Faber and Faber, 1966.
Larrissy, Edward, ed. *W. B. Yeats: Irish Writers in Their Time*. Dublin: Irish Academic, 2010.
Legge, James. *The Religions of China: Confucianism and Taoism Described and Compared with Christianity*. London: Hodder and Stoughton, 1880.
———. "Translator's Preface." In *I Ching: The Book of Changes*, xciii–ci. Translated by James Legge. New York: Bantam, 1969.
Lentricchia, Frank. *After the New Criticism*. London: Methuen, 1980.
Lindbeck, George. *The Nature of Doctrine: Religion and Theology in a Postliberal Age*. London: SPCK, 1984.
Liu, Lydia. *Translingual Practice: Literature, National Culture, and Translated Modernity— China, 1900–1937*. Stanford: Stanford University Press, 1995.
Liu Xiaogan. *Philosophy of Zhuangzi and Its Development*. Beijing: Peking University Press, 2010.
Lovell, Julia. "Evaluation on *The Critical Review*." *Morning Post*, February 1, 1922. Supplement.
———. "Introduction." In *The Real Story of Ah-Q and Other Tales of China*, by Lu Xun. Translated by Julia Lovell. Harmondsworth: Penguin, 2009.
———. *Jottings under Lamplight*. Edited by Eileen J. Cheng and Kirk A. Denton. Cambridge, MA: Harvard University Press, 2017.
———. *The Real Story of Ah-Q and Other Tales of China: The Complete Fiction of Lu Xun*. Translated by Julia Lovell. Harmondsworth: Penguin, 2009.
———. *Short History of Chinese Novels*. n.p., 1923.
Malins, Edward, and John Purkins, eds. *A Preface to Yeats*. 2nd ed. New York: Longman, 1994.
Marion, Jean-Luc. *Being Given: Towards a Phenomenology of Givenness*. Translated by Jeffrey L. Kosky. Stanford: Stanford University Press, 2002.
———. *In Excess: Studies of Saturated Phenomena*. Translated by Robyn Hormer. New York: Fordham University Press, 2002.
McCormack, W. J. *Blood Kindred: The Politics of W. B. Yeats and His Death*. London: Random House, 2005.
McFague, Sallie. *Speaking in Parables*. Philadelphia: Fortress, 1975.
Merrill, James. "Lost in Translation." *New Yorker*, April 8, 1974. 40.
Merton, Thomas. *The Way of Chuang Tzu*. New York: New Directions, 1965.
———. *The Way of Chuang Tzu*. Tunbridge Wells, Kent: Burns & Oates, 1995.
———. *The Wisdom of the Desert*. London: Sheldon, 1974.
Milton, John. *Paradise Lost*. n.p., 1667.
Mo Yan. "The Awakened Dream Teller: Random Thoughts on Yu Hua and His Fiction." In *Yu Hua 2000 Collection: Contemporary China Literature Reader*. Hong Kong: Ming Pao, 1999.
———. *Red Sorghum*. Translated by Howard Goldblatt. London: Arrow, 2003.
Müller, Friedrich Max, ed. *The Sacred Books of the East*. Vol. 39.1. Oxford: Clarendon, 1891.

Bibliography

Ou Guang-an. *Borrowing and Incorporation: Investigation on Yeats's Poetics*. Nankai: Nankai University Press, 2007.

———. *Classical and Modern Chinese: Case Studies of English–Chinese Translation in Modern China*. Nankai: Nankai University Press, 2017.

———. *Nation, Theme, Identity: Investigation Yeats's Poetry*. Nankai: Nankai University Press, 2006.

Oxford Dictionary of the Christian Church. 3rd ed. Edited by F. L. Cross and A. A. Livingstone. Oxford: Oxford University Press, 2005.

Pan-chiu Lai, and Jason Lam. *Sino-Christian Theology: A Theological Qua Cultural Movement in Contemporary China*. Frankfurt: Peter Lang, 2010

Pfister, Lauren F. *Striving for "The Whole Duty of Man": James Legge and the Scottish Protestant Encounter with China*. 2 vols. Berne: Peter Lang, 2004.

Purdy, Dwight Hilliard. *Biblical Echo and Allusion in the Poetry of William Butler Yeats: Poetics and the Art of God*. London: Associated University Press, 1994.

Pyper, Hugh. "The Reader in Pain: Job as Text and Pretext." In *Text as Pretext: Essays in Honour of Robert Davidson*, edited by Robert P. Carroll, 234–55. Sheffield: JSOT, 1992.

Qian Mu. *Collection of Annotations of Zhuangzi*. Beijing: SDX Joint, 2014.

Qian Zhongshu. "Introduction." In *Limited Views: Essays on Ideas and Letters by Qian Zhongshu*, translated by Ronald Egan. Cambridge, MA: Harvard University Asian Center, 1998.

———. *The Fortress Besieged*. Beijing: People's Literature, 2004.

———. "Preface." In *On the Art Poetry*, 3–5. Beijing: Commercial, 2016.

Ramet, Sabrina P. "Sacred Values and the Tapestry of Power: An Introduction." In *Render Unto Caesar: The Religious Sphere in World Politics*, edited by Sabrina P. Ramet and Donald W. Treadgold, 3–20. Washington DC: American University Press, 1995.

Records of the General Conference of Protestant Missionaries of China, Shanghai, May 10–24. Shanghai: Presbyterian Mission, 1878.

Ricoeur, Paul. *Oneself as Another*. Translated by Kathleen Blamey. Chicago: University of Chicago Press, 1992.

Rose, H. J. *A Handbook of Greek Mythology (Including Its Extension to Rome)*. London: Methuen, 1958.

Rosenthal, M. L. *Running to Paradise: Yeats's Poetic Art*. New York: Oxford University Press, 1994.

Ross, David. *Critical Companion to William Butler Yeats*. New York: Facts on File, 2009.

Sheng Keyi. *Death Fugue*. Artarmon, NSW: Giramondo, 2014.

———. *Northern Girls: Life Goes On*. Translated by Shelly Bryant. Beijing: Penguin China, 2015.

Shi-fu Huang, and Jiang Tie, eds. *A Comprehensive English–Chinese Dictionary*. Shanghai: Commercial, 1948

The Shorter Oxford English Dictionary on Historical Principles. 3rd ed. Oxford: Clarendon, 1964.

Shūsaku Endō. *Silence*. Translated by William Johnston. London: Peter Owen, 1969.

Simon, W. *A Beginner's Dictionary of the National Language (Gwoyeu)*. London: Percy Lund, Humphries, 1958.

Smith, Ann, ed. *The Novels of Thomas Hardy*. London: Vision, 1979.

Snaith, Norman H. *The Book of Job: Its Origin and Purpose*. London: SCM, 1968.

Spark, Muriel. *The Comforters*. 1957. Reprint, London: Virago, 2009.

Bibliography

———. *The Only Problem*. London: Triad Grafton, 1985.
Starr, Chloë. *Chinese Theology: Text and Context*. New Haven: Yale University Press, 2016.
———, ed. *Reading Christian Scriptures in China*. London: T & T Clark, 2008.
Steiner, George. *After Babel: Aspects of Language and Translation*. 2nd ed. Oxford: Oxford University Press, 1992.
———. "Foreword." In *Translating Religious Texts*, edited by David Jasper, x–xiv. London: Macmillan, 1993.
———. "A Note on Absolute Tragedy." *Literature and Theology* 4.2 (1990) 148.
Stock, Amy Geraldine. *W. B. Yeats: His Poetry and Thought*. Cambridge: Cambridge University Press, 1961.
Stowe, Harriet Beecher. *Uncle Tom's Cabin*. 1852. Ware: Wordsworth, 1995.
Süskind, Patrick. *Perfume*. Translated by John E. Woods. Harmondsworth: Penguin, 1987.
Synge, J. M. *The Playboy of the Western World*. n.p., 1907.
Tang Yan. *Qian Zhongshu*. Beijing: Cultural Development, 2019.
Todorov, Tzvetan. *Mikhail Bakhtin: The Dialogical Principle*. Translated by Wlad Godzic. Manchester: Manchester University Press, 1984.
Tomalin, Claire. *Thomas Hardy: The Time-Torn Man*. London: Viking, 2000.
Towler, Solala. "Introduction." *The Inner Chapters of Chuang Tzu*, by Chuang Tzu. London: Watkins, 2010.
Tuohy, Frank. *Yeats*. London: Macmillan London, 1976.
Unterecher, John. *A Reader's Guide to William Butler Yeats*. London: Thames and Hudson, 1965.
Vendler, Helen. *Our Secret Discipline: Yeats and Lyric Form*. Cambridge: Harvard University Press, 2007.
Waley, Arthur. *The Way and Its Power*. London: George Allen & Unwin, 1949.
Wang Bo. *The Philosophy of Zhuangzi*. Beijing: Peking University Press, 2004.
Wang Lixin. "Classic Quality and Methods in Research on Classic Studies and Oriental Literature—In Case of Classic Hebrew Literature." *Series of Oriental* 1 (2010) 28.
Webster, Harvey Curtis. *On a Darkling Plain*. London: Frank Cass, 1964.
Wellek, René, and Austin Warren. *Theory of Literature*. 1949. Reprint, Harmondsworth: Penguin, 1978.
Whyte, Bob. *Unfinished Encounter: China and Christianity*. London: Fount, 1988.
Willey, Basil. *More Nineteenth Century Studies: A Group of Honest Doubters*. London: Chatto & Windus, 1956.
Williams, Rowan. *Being Disciples*. London: SPCK, 2016.
Wilson, Edumund. *Axel's Castle: A Study in the Imaginative Literature of 1870–1931*. New York: Scriber's Sons, 1931.
Wong, Jenny. *The Translatability of the Religious Dimension in Shakespeare: From Page to Stage, from West to East*. Eugene, OR: Pickwick, 2018.
Wood, Michael. *Yeats and Violence*. New York: Oxford University Press, 2010.
Wu Leichuan. *Christianity and Chinese Culture*. Shanghai: Association Press of China of the YMCA, 1936.
———. *Christianity and Chinese Culture (Jiduhiao yu Zhongguo wenhua)*. 1936. Reprint, Shanghai: Shanghai Guji, 2008.
———. "Jesus as I Know Him." *Chinese Recorder* 61 (1930) 75–80.
Yan Lianke. *Dream of Ding Village*. Translated by Cindy Carter. London: Corsair, 2006.
———. *Serve the People!* Translated by Julia Lovell. London: Constable, 2007.

Bibliography

Yang Huilin. *China, Christianity, and the Question of Culture*. Waco, TX: Baylor University Press, 2014.

———. "The Value of Theology in the Humanities: Possible Approaches to Sino-Christian Theology." In *Sino-Christian Theology: A Theological Qua Cultural Movement in Contemporary China*, edited by Pan-chui Lai and Jason Lam. Frankfurt: Peter Lang, 2010.

Yang Huilin, and Daniel H. N. Yeung, eds. *Sino-Christian Studies in China*. Newcastle: Cambridge Scholars, 2006.

Yang Qiujuan. "Construction of National Cultural Identity: On Yeats's *The Wanderings of Oisin* and Others." *Feitian* 24 (2010) 49–50.

Yeats, W. B. *Autobiographies*. London: Macmillan, 1966.

———. *Collected Plays*. London: Macmillan, 1960.

———. *Collected Poems*. London: Macmillan, 1950.

———. *Explorations*. London: Macmillan, 1962.

———. *The Poems*. Edited by Daniel Albright. London: Everyman's Library, 1992.

———. *The Poems (A New Edition)*. Edited by Richard J. Finneran. London: Macmillan, 1984.

———. "The Preface." In *Selected Works of Yeats*, 1–14. Translated by Fu Hao. Beijing: Beijing Yanshan, 2008.

Yieh, John Y. H. "Reading the Sermon on the Mount in China: A Hermeneutical Enquiry into Its History of Reception." In *Reading Christian Scriptures in China*, edited by Chloë Starr, 143–62. London: T & T Clark, 2008.

Young, Edward J. *An Introduction to the Old Testament*. Translated by Daniel Chow et al. Hong Kong: Taosheng, 1977.

Yu Hua. *Chronicle of a Blood Merchant*. Translated by Andrew F. Jones. New York: Anchor, 2004.

———. *To Live*. Translated by Michael Berry. New York: Anchor, 2003.

Yuan Xingpei, ed. *History of Chinese Literature*. Vol. 1. Beijing: Higher Education, 1999.

Zhang Longxi. "Introduction." In *Patchwork: Seven Essays on Art and Literature by Qian Zhongshu*. Translated by Duncan M. Campbell. Leiden: Brill, 2014.

———. *From Comparison to World Literature*. New York: State University of New York Press, 2015.

Zhang Xiping, and Zhuo Xinping, eds. *The Exploration of Indigenization: A Collection of Studies on Christian Culture in the Twentieth Century*. Beijing: China Radio & Television 1999.

Zhu Weizhi. *Twelve Lectures on Biblical Literature*. Beijing: People's Literature, 1989.

Zhuangzi. *Zhuangzi*. Translated by Wang Rongpei. Changsha: Hunan; Beijing: Foreign Language, 1999.

———. *Zhuangzi*. Annotated by Fang Yong. Beijing: Zhonghua, 2010.

Ziolkowski, Eric. "Axial Age Theorizing and the Comparative Study of Religion and Literature." *Literature and Theology* 28.2 (2014) 129–50.

Index

A

Abbey Theatre, Dublin, 69, 73
Abraham, 25
Adam Bede (Eliot), 8, 141, 145, 153
Aeschylus, 34, 44, 57
Aesop, 105
After Babel (Steiner), 148, 151
Agamemnon (Aeschylus), 46
Altizer, Thomas, J. J., 125
Analects (Confucius), 14, 22, 49, 51, 104–5, 119, 138–39, 140
Answer to Job (Jung), 29–30
Apatheia, 19
Aristotle, 5
Auden, W. H., 62
Axial Age, 2–3, 24, 105, 133

B

Bakhtin, Mikhail, 14, 26, 67
Baldwin, Rev. S. L., 99
Barnhart Dictionary of Etymology, 43
Beggar Poems (Yeats), 71–72
Bell, Vereen M., 63
Bellah, Robert N., 3
Bian Zhilin, 102
Bible as Literature, The (Henn), 84
Biblical Echo and Allusion in the Poetry of William Butler Yeats (Purdy), 64
Binyon, Laurence, 57
Blake, William, 63, 83, 84, 85
Blanchot, Maurice, 5, 22, 124–25
Bloom, Harold, 63
Boethius, 43
Bonhoeffer, Dietrich, 94
Book of Common Prayer, The., 82–83
Book of God, The (Josipovici), 18, 30
Brief History of Chinese Philosophy (Feng Youlan), 104
Brooks, Cleanth, 62
Buddhism, 3
Byron, Lord, 57

C

Cambridge Companion to Modern Chinese Literature (Louie), 1
Cang Lang's Discussion on Poetry (Yan Yu), 103
Catholicism in Ireland, 64–81
Chaucer, Geoffrey, 43
Chichung Huang, 50, 51
China, Christianity, and the Question of Culture (Yang Huilin), 91
Chinese Academy of Social Sciences, Beijing, 91
Chinese Theology (Starr), 136–37
Christianity and Chinese Culture (Wu Leichuan), 92, 96, 124
Chronicle of a Blood Merchant (Yu Hua), 129–30
"Church and State" (Yeats), 75
Classical and Modern Chinese (Ou Guang-an), 148
Comforters, The (Spark), 31
Confucianism, 3, 14, 23, 35, 49, 52, 53, 92, 97, 98, 99, 118, 124, 142

Index

Confucius, 2, 8, 22, 24, 35, 51, 52, 92, 104–5, 109, 135, 138–39, 140
"Confucius in Modern China" (Lu Xun), 117
Consolation of Philosophy, The (Boethius), 43
"Coole and Ballylee" (Yeats), 75, 80
Coole Park (Ireland), 70, 75–76, 77, 78, 80
Crazy Jane Poems (Yeats), 74
Cullingford, Elizabeth, 63
Cultural Christians, 89, 90, 92, 136
Cultural Revolution, 90, 94–95, 97, 128, 131, 136
Culture and the Death of God (Eagleton), 6

D

Daodejing, 13, 23–24, 28, 53, 95, 159
Daoism (Taoism), 3, 8, 13, 16–23, 30, 35, 49, 52–54, 100, 105, 128, 135, 138, 139, 140, 142, 159
Darwin, Charles, 65
Death Fugue (Sheng Keyi), 132
Din Cheuk Lau, 50
Dostoyevsky, Fyodor, 32
Dream of Ding Village (Yan Lianke), 130
Dream of Red Mansions (*The Story of the Stone*), 8, 110
Dynasts, The (Hardy), 57

E

Eagleton, Terry, 6
"Easter, 1916" (Yeats), 72
Eliot, George, 8, 141, 153
Eliot, T. S., 61
Ellmann, R., 62, 64
Endo, Shūsako, 4
Ex Illa Dei (Papal Bull), 99
Explorations (Yeats), 85

F

Fang Yong, 21

Fate, 23, 41–55
Faulkner, William, 154
Fictions from Abroad (Lu Xun, Zhou Zuoren), 110
Finnegans Wake (Joyce), 151
Forster, R. F., 63
Fortress Besieged (Qian Zhongshu), 157
Foucault, Michel, 117, 127
Frank, William, 124
From Comparison to World Literature (Zhang Longxi), 4
Frost, Robert, 8
Fu Hao, 64

G

Gadamer, Hans-Georg, 94
Gao Xingjian, 133, 134, 135, 141–42, 145–47, 149, 153–54
Geng Youzhuang, 100
Giles, Herbert, 1, 3, 150
Gonne, Maude, 73
Good Soldier Svejk, The (Hašek), 5, 130
Green Helmet and Other Poems, The (Yeats), 71
Gregory, Lady, 69, 70, 78, 80
Guo Xiang, 13
Gutiérrez, Gustavo, 126, 133–34

H

Hardy, Florence, 57, 60
Hardy, Thomas, 5, 34–60, 81, 83, 128
Hašek, Jaroslav, 5, 130
Henn, T. R., 84.
History of Chinese Literature (Giles), 1
Hölderlin, Friedrich, 125
Holocaust, 94–95, 136
Howes, Marjorie, 63
Hu Shi, 155
Huxley, Thomas, Henry, 65

I

I Ching: The Book of Changes, 147

Index

Institute of Sino-Christian Studies (Tao Fong Shan), 2, 89
Irish Potato Famine, 77, 79

J

James, Henry, 56
Jaspers, Karl, 3, 24, 25, 29, 105, 133
Jeffares, A. Norman, 62
Job, the Book of, 7, 13–33, 149, 159
John, Gospel of, 28.
Jones, Andrew F., 130
Josipovici, Gabriel, 18, 30, 32
Journey to the West (Wu Cheng-en), 142, 153
Jude the Obscure (Hardy), 41, 58
Jung, Carl, 29

K

Kafka, Franz, 125
King Lear (Shakespeare), 37, 58
Klostermeier, Klaus, 151
Knight, G. Wilson, 58

L

"Lake Isle of Innisfree, The" (Yeats), 66
Lam, Jason, 90
Laozi, 8, 13, 19, 22, 23, 53, 54
Larkin, Philip, 83
"Leda and the Swan" (Yeats), 36
Lee, Mabel, 146
Legge, James, 2, 15, 16–17, 20–21, 23, 27, 49–50, 52, 91, 99, 100–01, 138–39, 147, 149, 159
Li Hongzhang, 119
Life of Thomas Hardy, The (Florence Hardy), 57
Lin Shu, 109
Lindbeck, George, 4, 91, 125, 134
Liu Tinfang, 92
Liu Xiaofeng, 89
Liu Xiaogan, 21
Logos, 28
Lonely Tower, The (Henn), 84

Lo Ping Cheung (Luo Bingxiang), 90–91
Louie, Kam, 1–2
Lovell, Julia, 110, 127
Lu Xun, 5, 6, 108–22, 126–28, 137, 138, 141, 155–57

M

MacBride, John ("Foxy Jack"), 72–73
Maignot, Charles, 98
Mao Zedong, 93–94, 109, 112, 128, 150, 151
Marion, Jean-Luc, 125, 135
Márquez, García, 154
Mayor of Casterbridge, The (Hardy), 41, 43, 47, 58
McFague, Sallie, 131
Melville, Hermann, 30
Mencius, 14, 147–48
Merchant of Venice, The (Shakespeare), 150
Merton, Thomas, 19, 128
Milton, John, 25, 59
"Minor Incident, A" (Lu Xun), 114–15, 121
Mo Yan, 129, 154
Mo-zi, 24
Mu Dan, 148
Müller, Max, 15

N

Nature of Doctrine (Lindbeck), 4, 91, 125, 134
New Cultural Movement, 155, 157
Nietzsche, Friedrich, 83, 85
North Ship, The (Larkin), 83
Northern Girls: Life Goes On (Sheng Keyi), 132–33
Norton Anthology of World Literature, The, 109

O

Odyssey, The (Homer), 7
Oedipus the King (Sophocles), 45, 46

Index

Old Man and the Sea, The (Hemingway), 120, 141
On the Art of Poetry (Qian Zhongshu), 158
Only Problem, The (Spark), 30–31, 32
Origin and Goal of History, The (Jaspers), 3, 24, 29
Outcry (Lu Xun), 108, 156
Outline of Chinese History of Philosophy (Hu Shi), 104

P

Paradise Lost (Milton), 25, 40, 59
Parnell, Charles, Stewart, 68, 71, 78
Patrick, St., 66–68, 74–75, 85
"Paudeen" (Yeats), 71
Perfume (Süskind), 111, 126
Permanence of Yeats, The (Hall and Steinman), 62
Pfister, Lauren, 101
Playboy of the Western World, The (Synge), 68–69
Poetics (Aristotle), 57
Poetics of Translation, A (Jasper, Geng, Wang), 100
Pound, Ezra, 61
Prodigal Son, Parable of the, 131, 132
Prometheus Bound (Aeschylus), 34, 44, 57
Protestantism in Ireland, 64–81
Psalms, Book of, 29, 31
Purgatory (Yeats), 82–83
Pyper, Hugh, 31

Q

Qian Mu, 21
Qian Zhongshu, 157–58

R

Rabelais, François, 130
Real Story of Ah-Q, The (Lu Xun), 5, 110–11, 120–21, 122, 126–27, 141, 156
Reicheldt, Karl Ludwig, 2

Religion in Human Evolution (Bellah), 3
Religions of China, The (Legge), 2, 17, 27, 159
Rémusat, M. Abel, 28
Renmin University of China, 89, 98–99, 101, 149
Researches into the Early History of Mankind (Tylor), 27
Responsibilities (Yeats), 71, 77
Ribh Poems (Yeats), 74
Ricci, Matteo, 91, 98–99, 101, 149
"Rose Tree, The" (Yeats), 73, 79
Russell, Bertrand, 157

S

Sacred Books of the East (Müller), 15
Saturated phenomenon, 126, 135, 137
Saussure, Ferdinand de, 157
Scottish Enlightenment, 101
Scriptural Reasoning, 14, 28, 99–100, 101, 105
"September, 1914" (Yeats), 69
Serve the People! (Yan Lianke), 5, 130–32
Shakespeare, William, 1, 8, 151
Shanghai Missionary Conference (1877), 99
Shelley, Percy Bysshe, 57, 63
Sheng Keyi, 5, 132–33
Short History of Chinese Novels (Lu Xun), 122
Silence (Endo), 4, 126
Sino- Christian Studies in China (Yang and Yeung), 89, 91
Sino-Christian Theology, 89–107, 123–24, 135, 136, 158–59
Sino-Christian Theology: A Theological Qua Cultural Movement (Lai and Lam) 97, 123
"Sixteen Dead Men" (Yeats), 73, 79
Solomon, 25
Soothill, William Edward, 49–50

Index

Soul Mountain (Gao Xingjian), 133, 135, 141–42, 145–46, 149, 151, 153–54
Spark, Muriel, 30–31, 32
Spirituality, 117, 119–20, 139–42, 156
Starr, Chloë, 96–97, 136–37
Steiner, George, 8, 148–49, 151
Stevenson, Robert Louis, 56
Stock, Amy Geraldine, 63
Supernatural Songs (Yeats), 85
Synge, J. M., 68–69
Szekar Wan, 96

T

Talmud, 30
Tao Te Ching, See *Daodejing*
Taoism, See Daoism
Term Question, 149
Tess of the D'Urbervilles (Hardy), 5, 34–60, 128
Texts of Taoism, The (Legge), 100
Theology of Literature, A (Franke), 124
Theory of Literature (Wellek and Warren), 102
"This is What I Meant" (Lu Xun), 112–13
Thomas, Dylan, 83
Three Self Movement, 93
Timon of Athens (Shakespeare), 58
"To a Shade" (Yeats), 71
To Live (Yu Hua), 59, 128–30
Tomalin, Claire, 59
Translatability of the Religious Dimension in Shakespeare, The (Wong), 150
Translating Religious Texts (Jasper), 148
Troilus and Criseyde (Chaucer), 43
Tylor, Sir Edward, 27

U

Ulysses (Joyce), 141, 151, 154
Uncle Tom's Cabin (Stowe), 109
Under the Volcano (Lowry), 115

"Upstairs in the Tavern" (Lu Xun), 115–16

V

Vita Nova (Lu Xun et al), 108, 127–28

W

Waley, Arthur, 23, 139
"Wanderings of Oisin, The" (Yeats), 66–68
Wang Chong, 140
Wang, David Der-Wei, 113
Wang Hai, 22, 100
Watkins, Vernon, 83
Way of Chuang Tzu, The (Merton), 19, 128
Wiesel, Elie, 95
"Wild Swans at Coole, The" (Yeats), 70
William of Orange, 77
Willey, Basil, 57
Wilson, Angus, 62
Wittgenstein, Ludwig, 32
Wong, Jenny, 149–50
Wu Leichuan, 92, 95–97, 98, 124
Wu Mi, 148, 154
Wuwei (doing nothing), 22, 59, 128

X

Xunzi, 52

Y

Yan Lianke, 5, 130–32, 134
Yang Huilin, 89, 91, 92, 93, 94, 95, 99–100, 136
Yeats (Bloom), 63
Yeats, John Butler, 65, 80
Yeats, W. B., 5, 6, 36, 61–86, 152
Yeo Khiok-Khng, 98
Yeung, Daniel, 89
Yu Hua, 5, 59, 128–30

Index

Z

Zeng Dian, 104, 105
Zhang Longxi, 4, 109, 124, 133
Zhao Jing, 100
Zhao Zichen, 92
Zhou Zuoren, 110, 127
Zhuangzi, 13–33, 41, 140
Zhuangzi (Chuang Tzu), 13–33, 139–40, 159